Teaching Second Language Listening

Also published in
Oxford Handbooks for Language Teachers

Teaching American English Pronunciation
Peter Avery and Susan Ehrlich

ESOL: A Critical Guide
Melanie Cooke and James Simpson

Success in English Teaching
Paul Davies and Eric Pearse

Doing Second Language Research
James Dean Brown and Theodore S. Rodgers

Teaching Business English
Mark Ellis and Christine Johnson

Intercultural Business Communication
Robert Gibson

Teaching and Learning in the Language Classroom
Tricia Hedge

Teaching Second Language Reading
Thom Hudson

Teaching English Overseas: An Introduction
Sandra Lee McKay

Teaching English as an International Language
Sandra Lee McKay

How Languages are Learned (3rd edition)
Patsy M. Lightbown and Nina Spada

Communication in the Language Classroom
Tony Lynch

Teaching Young Language Learners
Annamaria Pinter

The Oxford ESOL Handbook
Philida Schellekens

Doing Task-based Teaching
Jane Willis and Dave Willis

Explaining English Grammar
George Yule

Teaching Second Language Listening

TONY LYNCH

OXFORD
UNIVERSITY PRESS

OXFORD
UNIVERSITY PRESS

Great Clarendon Street, Oxford ox2 6DP

Oxford University Press is a department of the University of Oxford.
It furthers the University's objective of excellence in research, scholarship,
and education by publishing worldwide in

Oxford New York

Auckland Cape Town Dar es Salaam Hong Kong Karachi
Kuala Lumpur Madrid Melbourne Mexico City Nairobi
New Delhi Shanghai Taipei Toronto

With offices in

Argentina Austria Brazil Chile Czech Republic France Greece
Guatemala Hungary Italy Japan Poland Portugal Singapore
South Korea Switzerland Thailand Turkey Ukraine Vietnam

OXFORD and OXFORD ENGLISH are registered trade mark of
Oxford University Press in the UK and in certain other countries

© Oxford University Press 2009

The moral rights of the authors have been asserted

Database right Oxford University Press (maker)

First published 2009
2015
10 9 8 7 6 5

ISBN 978 0 19 442334 2

Typeset by SPI Publisher Services, Pondicherry, India

Printed in China

Dedico este libro a la gente de La Ablaneda y de Les Cuendies

CONTENTS

ACKNOWLEDGEMENTS

I was fortunate in having some excellent teachers of French and German at Collyer's Grammar School, Horsham—R.W. Kenyon, John Gosney, and Peter Collins. I hope that if they had read this book they would have recognized where listening to them eventually led me. I have also gained a lot from less formal tuition from Heinzel Langer, Jos Hollenbrand, Maggi Thegström, Kerstin Sars, Mauricéa Lima Lynch, and Nivaldo Bezerra de Lima. As a young language student, I was welcomed into various European homes, among them those of the Manz and Ongsieck families (Baden Baden), the Borsches (Oberursel), the Binoches (Sainte-Marie-sur-Mer), the Charpentiers (Hauho), and the Noormans (Leeuwarden). I thank them all for their hospitality and friendship.

Like others, I owe a great deal to Professor Gillian Brown of Clare College, University of Cambridge, who was one of an outstanding group of lecturers in the late Department of Applied Linguistics at the University of Edinburgh and who inspired a lasting fascination with the language that we hear around us. The period I subsequently spent working with her and Anne Anderson on the Scottish Education Department project on listening comprehension skills in 1983–1984 stimulated my interest in the ways in which people listen to (or ignore) each other when the communicative going gets tough.

I would like to thank the many people I have worked with at the Institute for Applied Language Studies at Edinburgh since 1980, in particular Kenneth Anderson, Gillian D. Brown, Clive Criper, Eric Glendinning, Joan Maclean, and Hugh Trappes-Lomax. One sub-group at IALS deserves special mention—Kenneth Anderson, Cathy Benson, Pauline Gillies, Anne Heller-Murphy, Cathy Holden, and Brian Parkinson—who have shared Workroom 3.3 with me for up to a quarter of a century and in whose conversations I have participated as addressee, auditor, overhearer, and, occasionally, judge.

My thanks also go to the IALS colleagues who contributed to this book by giving me their interpretations of the restaurant text featured in Chapter 4: Aida Fernandez Lopez, Anne Heller-Murphy, Atsuko Moriyama, Camilla Green, Cathy Benson, Christine Frayling-Kelly, Elisabeth McCulloch,

Florence Dégeilh, Isabel Hurtado de Mendoza, Jacqueline Gollin, and Roser Vich Gallego.

The final shape of the book owes a great deal to the skills of the editorial team at Oxford University Press, particularly Cristina Whitecross, Julia Bell, Natasha Forrest, and Catherine Kneafsey.

The author and publisher are grateful to those who have given permission to reproduce the following extracts and adaptations of copyright material:

p.10 Figure entitled 'Model of a communication system' by C. Shannon from *The Mathematical Theory of Communication* by Claude E. Shannon and Warren Weaver. Copyright 1949, 1998 by the Board of Trustees of the University of Illinois. Used with permission of the author and the University of Illinois Press.

p.12 Figure entitled 'An information processing model of comprehension' by A. Maley from *Second Selections from Modern English Teacher*. Copyright of Alan Maley. Published by Longman Publishers. Reproduced by kind permission of Alan Maley.

p.30 Figure entitled 'A model of spoken communication' from *The Architecture of Normal Spoken Language Use* by W. Levelt. Reproduced by kind permission of Mouton de Gruyter, a division of Walter de Gruyter & Co.

p.33 Table entitled 'Enabling skills and enacting skills in listening' by M. Rost from *Listening in Language Learning*. Reproduced by kind permission of Pearson Education Limited.

p.61 Table entitled 'A participation framework for listening' by A. Bell from *Language in Society*. Reproduced by kind permission of Cambridge University Press.

p.89 Table entitled 'Checklist for integrating the Macrostrategies' by Tony Lynch from *Study Listening*. Reproduced by kind permission of Cambridge University Press.

p.96 Figure entitled 'Model of second language listening comprehension' by J. Flowerdew and L. Miller from *Second Language Listening*. Reproduced by kind permission of Cambridge University Press.

Although every effort has been made to trace and contact copyright holders before publication, this has not been possible in some cases. We apologize for any apparent infringement of copyright and, if notified, the publisher will be pleased to rectify any errors or omissions at the earliest opportunity.

PREFACE:
A LISTENER'S HISTORY

At various points in the book I will be using examples from my own listening experiences, in English and other languages, to illustrate how general principles translate into particular cases. The way in which any of us listen to other people and other languages is inevitably shaped by our individual listening histories and the specific contexts in which we have encountered a language. To provide you with some of the background that has shaped me as a listener, I will briefly summarize my 'career' in listening.

English

My first memory of encountering a problem in understanding spoken English is of a day in 1955 when I was playing in the fields near my parents' house in Horsham, in the south of England. I became aware of an unfamiliar face peering at me through a clump of tall grass. The face's owner was a boy of about my size. After a few seconds he said, 'Wot ear jar ye?' I had no idea what language this was. The boy repeated, 'Wot ear jar ye?' and then helpfully reformulated that as 'High all dar ye?' 'I'm six', I replied. 'Aim seven', he said in triumph and ran off. I later learnt that his name was Peter and his parents had just moved to our road from a place called Ulster. I remember asking my mother what language they spoke in Ulster and not believing her when she insisted it was English.

French

I started French at the local grammar school, where our teacher had some difficulty managing the new reel-to-reel recorder. So we spent quite a lot of time listening to French played at high speed, both forwards and backwards, while he looked for the right place on the reel. My first encounter with real spoken French came when I spent three weeks on an exchange with Emmanuel, a doctor's son from Paris, at his family's holiday home on the coast of Brittany. There I spent most days on the beach chatting to Emmanuel's friends, who were also mainly holiday homers. This meant I heard a wide variety of French accents, but in fact it was my lack of vocabulary that was the main problem in understanding spoken French. Emmanuel's friends did their best to ensure that I picked up some contemporary slang. On the way back to the house for lunch each day, Emmanuel would ask me what words I had been taught that morning and would tell me which ones I was not to use in front of his parents.

Latin

I studied Latin throughout my seven years at grammar school, but for the first three or four years any 'listening' we did was limited to hearing other boys read out the sentences they had translated into Latin and then hearing the teacher give the correct answer. In the later years, when we were more advanced, he also used to read aloud classical poems and our set texts, but when he did we always had the printed text in front of us. We never 'simply' listened; listening to and reading Latin were effectively a combined activity, with listening very much the junior partner.

German

In my third year at grammar school I chose to do German, mainly because my father spoke it fluently. He had done some German evening classes just before the Second World War, enlisted in the Royal Artillery and was captured on Crete in 1941. He then spent four years as a prisoner of war in Steiermark, Austria, where he acquired the local dialect through working as an interpreter in his prison camp and as a farm labourer in the summer months. After the war he kept in touch with several of the people he had worked for, and with one couple in particular, the Auers. So when I started German, I began to write letters to Frau Auer as additional practice, spending hours deciphering the Gothic handwriting in her replies. In 1965 we went to Steiermark on a family holiday, where I realized for the first time the marked differences between spoken and written German. I remember, for example, that the Auers pronounced the word *eins* (one) rather like the Welsh name Owens, and that when they said things were 'very good' they said /seər guət/ rather than the standard German /zeər gut/ that we used at school. Later, before going to university in 1968, I spent three months working in the office of a chemical company in a small village near Baden Baden in south-west Germany, where I stayed with a local couple who spoke only the Badish dialect in two forms—fast and slower. But I did not see these differences as a problem—I thought they were great fun and made listening to German more interesting.

Swedish

I studied German and French at the University of Cambridge, and during my first year the local Arts cinema put on a short season of Ingmar Bergman films, shown in Swedish with English subtitles. I saw five or six of the Bergman classics and remember being fascinated by the fact that, although Swedish could occasionally sound quite like German, most of the time it sounded completely different. Words such as the Swedish *man* and German *Mann* (man) were practically the same, but not other words such as *kvinna* and *Frau* (woman). I bought a *Teach Yourself Swedish* book and studied its vocabulary and grammar—this was the age before audiocassettes. During my second Cambridge summer vacation I worked for six weeks in a factory in Skåne, the southernmost province of Sweden. I had only ever heard Swedish spoken by Bergman's actors, which turned out to be inadequate preparation for understanding the factory foreman's Skånska accent. Faced with my non-comprehension, the poor man was forced to make ever greater adjustments to his Swedish to accommodate to my level of listening. This was my first conscious experience of hearing someone using marked 'foreigner talk' to me, in the cause of communication. After leaving Cambridge I taught English for two years in Sweden with the British Centre: one year in Falun and the second in Umeå. My main reason for going there was to improve my Swedish, but British Centre teachers were supposed to use only English in class, so I spent two years pretending *not* to understand what my students were saying to each other in Swedish—the opposite of the more usual second language listening situation.

Finnish

After working in the Skåne factory I spent an idyllic four weeks in the autumn of 1970 on a farm near Hauho in southern Finland, which gave me a smattering of Finnish. At that time the Finnish government was encouraging native speakers of English to go to stay or work with Finnish families to help raise the standard of English spoken by the older generations, who had not had the opportunity to do English at school. I chose to stay with a farming family and spent the days doing various jobs around the farm, picking fruit and collecting perch and pike from the nets in the farm's many lakes. My main Finnish listening task each day was to understand the farm foreman's single-word instruction; to this day I remember *mustikka* (bilberry), *puolukka* (cranberry), *peruna* (potato), and *kala* (fish).

Dutch

My limited Dutch comes partly from conversations with Jos, a student I worked with in the Swedish factory, but mainly from six weeks' teaching practice in Leeuwarden in the north of the Netherlands in 1974. There I stayed with two English teachers, Jaap and Anke, and their three-year-old daughter Aukje. I decided Aukje would make an excellent informal Dutch tutor, so I asked her lots of questions about vocabulary—mostly on the lines of 'What's this?' and 'What do you call that?'. Things went rather well, I thought, until one day her father said there was something odd about the way I spoke Dutch—not an accent exactly, just something about my intonation. A day or so later he heard Aukje talking to me and was able to put his finger on the problem: I had been imitating the intonation of her answers to my continual questions about words, in which she expressed the amazement with which a three-year-old reacts to an apparently mature adult who does not know the names of even the simplest everyday objects.

Portuguese

The next place I taught abroad was Porto in Portugal, where I worked for nine months in 1974–1975 and picked up enough Portuguese to get by. I later met my wife Mauricéa, who is from Recife in north-east Brazil, where we spent a year in 1979–1980 and have been on visits since. Having got used to the heavily elided vowels of the Portuguese of northern Portugal, I found it quite hard at first to understand Brazilian Portuguese, particularly the accents of Rio de Janeiro and São Paulo that tend to predominate on television and radio. But the fact that Mauricéa is a native speaker means that in Brazil and Portugal I am often able to slip into the role of 'listener-in' during her transactions in offices and shops, and to some extent in conversations with friends and family. This is a privileged role for the informal learner, because it brings the benefit of exposure to large amounts of **comprehensible input**, without the requirement to produce much spoken output.

Spanish

My latest, and perhaps last, language is Spanish. We bought a house in a village in Asturias in northern Spain in 2004, since when I have been combining formal study of Spanish in evening classes in Edinburgh and plenty of speaking practice every three months or so, when we go to Asturias. So Spanish is the language I am now practising and listening to most, in official settings like the local town hall, in discussions with our builder, in shops and—most of all—in conversations with our neighbours. Beginning another language at the age of 55 has been a useful reminder for me of what second language listening involves for learners at lower levels of proficiency in the language, and has renewed my enthusiasm for devising ways of helping my students in Edinburgh to cope with spoken English.

So the main things that my particular listening history has made me aware of in these different contexts are:

- the variation among regional accents
- the difference between spoken and written forms of a language
- the importance of an extensive 'recognition vocabulary' for effective listening
- the key role of intonation for more nuanced communication
- the ways in which native speakers may accommodate to foreign listeners
- the benefits of plentiful comprehensible input
- the intricacies of combined listening and speaking, in face-to-face interaction in a second language.

More generally, I am aware that learning and acquiring other languages represents a rich source of first-hand experience for me to exploit in the listening classroom—particularly incidents in which I have misheard or misinterpreted what someone has said. I will be using some of those incidents during the course of the book to illustrate the complexities of what we have to do when listening to a second language.

PART ONE

Background issues

1 LISTENING: 21st CENTURY PERSPECTIVES

Introductory task

Each chapter in this book opens with a task that invites you to reflect on a listening issue in the light of your own experience as a listener. This first task is based on an incident that I will be revisiting in Chapter 2. It happened one afternoon when I was at home in Edinburgh with my wife and some Brazilian friends—mother, father, and three children. It involved the youngest child, who was about five years old. Our conversation was in Portuguese, so what you are about to read is a translation of what I thought I heard.

GIRL   (*looking at Mauricéa*) Do you have my cup?
            (*Everyone laughs—except me*).
MOTHER   Oh, I'm going to die of embarrassment!
GIRL   Do you have my cup here?
MAURICÉA   Yes. Let's go and find one.
            (*Mauricéa and the little girl leave the room. They come back a minute or so later. The girl is carrying a plate with a tangerine on it.*)
            (*Everyone laughs, and this time I join in, though still puzzled.*)

Why do you think the people laughed? What do you think made me join in the laughter the second time? (You will find answers towards the end of Chapter 2.)

Introduction

Even in our first language we can face considerable obstacles to understanding speech. Comprehension may be made more difficult by any of a variety of factors inside our head: internal distractions (such as emotional upset or toothache), lack of interest, emotional reaction to the speaker or topic, jumping to conclusions, over-reacting to the language the speaker uses, and preparing a response to what the speaker has said. When listening in a second language there are likely to be additional problems:

the expressions the speaker chooses, their speed of speaking, unfamiliar content and cultural references, and so on. It is no wonder that the terms used in the listening literature to characterize the process of coping with second language speech often emphasize physical pressure ('load', 'burden', 'barrier', 'obstacle'), the transient nature of speech ('transitory', 'ephemeral', 'temporary'), lack of clarity ('buzz', 'fog', 'fuzzy', and 'blur'), and the listener's sense of being overwhelmed (by the 'stream', 'flood', 'torrent', 'cascade').

Listeners and listening

In this book I want to place the listener at centre stage. What interests me as a language teacher is not so much the listening process itself, but rather how we can use our growing understanding of that process to help our students to become better listeners. Any book with 'listening' in its title tends to imply that there is a single proper or correct way of understanding spoken language. In fact, there are different 'listenings', so to speak—different ways and purposes of listening; there are also countless individuals doing those listenings; and the same individual will listen in different ways under differing circumstances. So in this book I will be discussing academic research into listening that has led to general conclusions about how people listen to a second language, but I will also be using specific instances of misunderstanding, or delayed understanding, which throw light on listening processes at the individual level.

Invisibility

The notion of 'throwing light on' something has a specific relevance to listening. As many authors have pointed out, listening is a largely hidden process and may have no observable product or outcome. Even when a listener does provide a visible or audible response that suggests successful comprehension, such as a nod or 'uh-huh', there is no guarantee that they have actually understood what the speaker meant. The listener may not even realize they have misheard or misinterpreted. They might also want to disguise the fact that they know they have not grasped the point.

> We cannot base our analysis completely on what we judge, from the discourse, to be comprehended by the non-native speaker. The determination of comprehension is, in fact, quite elusive. (Hawkins 1985: 176)

In Chapter 5 I will be discussing some of the social pressures on second language users that can lead them to conceal their non-comprehension—as I did in the Portuguese 'cup' incident in the Introductory Task.

Complexity

Listening comprises several dimensions of complexity. Firstly, the processes of listening themselves can be complex, even if we seem to manage them quite successfully most of the time—at least in our own language, or a second language in which we have become proficient. The second sort of complexity arises from increasingly sophisticated twenty-first century computer technology, which is something of a double-edged sword: on the one hand, the technology is making it possible for second language learners to do more listening to more languages at less cost than ever before; on the other, for language teachers, accessing and using the technology makes ever growing demands on our professional and technical skills. Thirdly, conducting effective research into listening is also complex, given the number of factors that stand in the researchers' way, such as the inaccessibility of what goes on in listeners' heads and the variety of influences on the success or failure of attempts to understand spoken language. In the next three sections of this chapter I sample those three perspectives on listening complexity: the lived experiences of listeners, the potential of electronic media, and researchers' theories of listening.

Listeners

Below are four sets of comments which give a flavour of the different ways in which individuals incorporate listening into their lives, both in their own language and in other languages.

The radio fan

> I have BBC Radio 4 on most of the time. In fact, we have a radio in every room of our flat, including the bathroom. The one by the bed comes on before I get up; my day begins with the Today programme and ends with the midnight news. When we're cooking or doing the washing up, we always have the radio on, and when we come back from somewhere like work or shopping, almost the first thing I do is turn on the radio in the kitchen. So it's normally the spoken word we have on in the background, mainly Radio 4, but I even listen to football commentaries and phone-ins on Radio 5. My wife draws the line at that. The only exception is when I'm working on the computer—if I listen to people speaking, I find it interferes with my thinking. It's the same with songs. If I have music on when I'm working it has to be instrumental stuff, not songs, otherwise I listen to the lyrics and can't think properly. So for me the radio is just an important part of the background and I can't really imagine being in the flat without it on. They do say that the pictures are better on radio, don't they?

The TV viewer

> I seem to watch a lot more TV than the teachers I work with. I often seem to be the only person who's seen a particular programme. Or perhaps they just don't want to admit it? But I find that with some sorts of programmes it's hard for me to watch as an ordinary viewer. I can't switch off from being a language teacher. I sometimes find myself looking through the TV listings for material I can use

with a particular group of students. In science programmes or documentaries, on something like carbon capture for instance, I tend to monitor the voice-over, or the people being interviewed, for the expressions they're using, and to watch how I reckon the visual information would help a listener understand the point. And I also listen out for language clues in what's being said that may mark Situation-Problem-Solution-Evaluation structure, like 'One possible answer...' for Solution, or 'But whether...' for Evaluation. I don't know whether all this is really normal, even for a language teacher!

The iPod owner

Mainly I want to hear music in my iPod but I do use the radio, too, to improve my English listening. I like programmes which give a transcript on the BBC website. I first listen and sometimes write down some notes. I can listen to what the people in the programme say and then I can check my notes with the website. I sometimes listen to the text again and again, like children do, and even repeat the words of the reporters to try to remember useful phrases. Downloading to my iPod lets me listen again to programmes on the bus or when I'm at home, in parallel with my regular routines like cooking and cleaning. I have also experimented with 'just' hearing, not listening, not concentrating on special words but to get English inside my head. Having it there inside is quite different. It makes me feel like I'm understanding more.

The laptop user

I like watching DVD films on my laptop. One of my Spanish classmates offered us a selection of films and I chose some that seemed interesting. It's good to have the subtitles there if I need them, but I don't normally read them. I concentrate on what the actors are saying and if there's something I haven't caught, or I think I must have misheard, then I look at the subtitles. Some people say the sound quality isn't very good on DVD but I've found it OK. Sometimes I do replay bits where I want to get the exact structure or expression. DVDs are a good way to get familiar with different accents. One film I watched was Motorcycle Diaries, which is about two young men from Argentina who go by motorbike through South America, so that had a variety of accents in it. But I really watch DVDs mainly for enjoyment. I don't retain very much from any one film, not consciously anyway, but I think it helps consolidate what I already know.

Technologies

The rapid development of electronic media over the last 30 years gives us access to a wider range of voices in other languages. Strong claims have been made for the benefits of the novel facilities offered in computer-enhanced language learning (CELL) materials; for example, that

> the computer and interactive technologies will allow teachers to select materials of all kinds, support them as learners' needs dictate, and use the visual options

of screen presentation or the interactive capabilities of computer control to help students develop good listening techniques. (Garrett 1991: 95)

Each new generation of technology—the reel-to-reel recorder, the language laboratory, the audiocassette player, the video recorder, the DVD player, and the handheld computer—has excited predictions that *this* is the one that will bring really radical advances in language teaching. However, the hardware has tended to run ahead of the pedagogic purposes to which teachers might want to put it. There is no denying that CELL, the most recent case of medium innovation, has put second language listening experiences within the reach of many learners, but for the purposes of this book, the key question is: Has it actually changed the *ways* in which learners listen to second language speech? As we will see in later chapters, the *internal* processes of listening to and viewing material on computer are not radically different from watching the same event live, or on television, or via a video recorder or DVD player, even if the *social* processes may be different. Indeed, in a recent article on the value of multimedia software in the teaching of listening skills, Jan Hulstijn of the University of Amsterdam went so far as to argue that the major milestone in the history of second language listening instruction was *not* the arrival of modern digital multimedia technology, 'but rather the invention, more than 100 years ago, of the phonograph and similar devices with which sound could be recorded, stored, played and replayed' (Hulstijn 2003: 420). What twenty-first century CELL technology offers is simply a more convenient way of delivering spoken language to learners than was available in previous technologies.

Debra Hoven of the University of Queensland made a similar point about the ways in which teachers use CELL materials for listening and viewing comprehension:

Although the presence of new technology and new means of using it entail the development of new models [of second language instruction], there is no reason to start completely afresh. (Hoven 1999: 88)

Text	Audio	Video	Computer
The **text/tapescript** shows …	The **soundtrack** adds …	The **video image** adds …	The **computer** adds …
words spoken	**voice(s)**	**speakers' bodies** – gestures – facial expressions	**learner control** – precision of replay – flexibility of support – choice of media (DVD, iPod)
'stage directions' – accompanying actions – emotion in the voice	**prosodic elements** – intonation – pitch – stress – accent(s) **audible context** – sounds off – 'atmosphere'	**visible context** – general setting – actions/movement – deictic reference	**support options** – subtitles (first or second language) – hotlinks to word glosses – slower rate **online hyperlinks to** – dictionary – encyclopedia – corpora

Information available for use in comprehension

relative scarcity ◼◼◼◼◼◼◼ ◼ ◼ ◼ ◼ ◼ ◼ ◼ ◼ ◼ ◼ ◼ ◼ ◼ ◼ ◼ *relative wealth*

Table 1.1 The relationship between different media in listening comprehension

What the more 'advanced' technologies do is to complement, rather than replace, existing ones, as sketched in Table 1.1.

As we look from left to right in the table, we see a progressive increase in the amount of help available to the listener in understanding spoken language. The transcript of the words spoken (Text) gives a written version of what was said, but it is hard to convey the nuances; one would need the Audio medium to be able to appreciate, for example, the performances of two different actors working with the same script. The Video medium then adds the physical context in which the speaker is talking. While it might be difficult to tell from the soundtrack whether a speaker is being ironic, their facial expressions and body language might make that clear in the video version. Finally, the Computer puts at the listeners' disposal greater control over the playing of the original spoken material and extends the potential range of supporting data that may assist comprehension, such as subtitles and access to background resources.

Although a great deal is now technically possible, its pedagogic value has to be carefully evaluated. Does the combination of media actually help second language learners to listen more effectively? If so, does it help them to learn and retain over the longer term? Here we face a paradox: the availability of non-audio information, which makes it easier for the listener to *understand* what is said, may at the same time make it more difficult to *learn*. The learner with on-screen access to subtitles or transcript may not need to listen. We will come back to this in Chapters 7 and 10.

The strong claims made for (any) new technology have to be carefully assessed against the actual benefits to the second language learner. The advantages that have been claimed for multimedia materials are no exception. What we can say with certainty is that computers will offer second language listeners greater choice and control, and the opportunity to adapt listening materials to their own particular learning needs and preferred learning style in the following areas:

- *content*—what, and how much, to watch or listen to
- *mode*—video, audio or audio/video
- *activity*—whether or not to do a particular task as intended
- *task type*—comprehension or language awareness
- *difficulty*—choice between levels of task
- *support*—whether to access subtitles or hypertext
- *sequence*—which order to do tasks in
- *time and pace*—learner control over when to start, pause, and stop
- *advice*—whether to resort to online help in relation to the specific task or to language learning more generally.

(based on Brett 1995: 78)

Given the range of choices and options it makes available, multimedia listening offers a potential platform for teachers and learners to experiment with alternatives, and could help to make learners more aware of their personal learning processes and preferences—a point I will be coming back to in Chapters 10 and 11.

Theories

The driving force behind two main theories of listening since the 1950s—**Communication Theory** and **Information Processing**—was research into technologies of telecommunications and artificial intelligence, respectively. Those theories and a third, very different approach—**Social Constructivism**—reflect two important strands in the development of listening research over the last 60 years. Firstly, there has been a shift of focus from relying on experimentally observed comprehension towards an analysis of interaction in real social contexts. Secondly, there has been a marked change of overall approach from regarding comprehension as *reception*, which assigned an almost mechanical role to the human listener, to one that sees comprehension as *interpretation*, highlighting the part played by the listener as an active participant or agent in the communication process.

Communication Theory

Communication Theory (CT) or, more precisely, the Mathematical Theory of Communication (Shannon and Weaver 1949), developed from engineering research that was intended to increase the efficiency of telecommunications systems. The researchers represented communication as in Figure 1.1.

There we see terms that are still in regular use in describing listening processes: 'signal', 'message', and 'noise'. The fundamental notion of information in CT was statistical: the information value of any element of the message depended on its predictability in the sequence of bits of information. For example, once we have identified the initial elements of an English word as EXCHE, the rest can only be QUER. In CT terms the final syllable of the word is meaningless because it is entirely predictable.

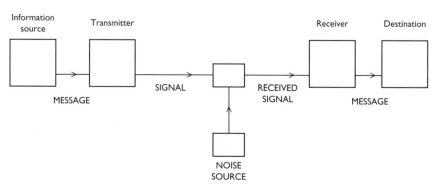

Figure 1.1 Model of a communication system (Shannon 1949: 5)

Notice that the human speaker and listener have peripheral roles, as 'information source' and 'destination'. Their participation does not affect the efficiency of the system itself: 'the concern was with intelligibility rather than perception, and the results were used to evaluate equipment rather than listeners' (Licklider and Miller 1951: 1040). Nevertheless, CT researchers addressed three levels of engineering problem that have been influential since: the technical problem—'How accurately can the symbols of communication be transmitted?'; the semantic problem—'How precisely do the transmitted symbols convey the desired meaning?'; and the effectiveness problem— 'How effectively does the received meaning affect conduct in the desired way?' (Shannon 1949: 9). These three aspects of comprehension would later form the basis of the Information Processing model of listening.

Information Processing

This second model was developed during the computer revolution of the 1970s and 1980s, in particular in research into artificial intelligence. Central to Information Processing (IP) are the elements of input, processing, and output. Human beings are limited processors and have to work within the constraints of our physical capacity to deal with incoming information. When we carry out complex tasks such as listening, we have to allocate more attention to one aspect of the task and less to another. IP is associated in particular with the American cognitive psychologist John Anderson, whose three-stage model of Perception, **Parsing**, and Utilization (Anderson 1985) reflects the three levels of problem addressed in CT: listeners have to *identify* what is being said, *interpret* what is being meant, and *respond* in an appropriate manner.

That is easier said than done, of course. When artificial intelligence researchers tried to write software that would enable computers to 'understand' messages like humans do, they found that even quite simple messages required the programming of enormous amounts of information. They drew on **schema theory** (which I discuss in Chapter 4) to describe how knowledge is structured in human memory and exploited in comprehension. As we try to make sense of what we hear, we use as wide a range of relevant mental resources as we have available. Figure 1.2 captures the essence of an IP model of listening.

This represents an advance on the earlier CT model. 'Input' now includes not just what is said, but also accompanying non-verbal information. 'Decoding' involves selecting the significant elements in what the listener hears. Some parts of the message are committed to short-term memory, but not all, since the memory system has very limited capacity. To compensate for that, the listener uses their knowledge of the language to predict how the current utterance will continue and to anticipate what the next will be about. In order to interpret what the speaker means and why they are saying it, the listener

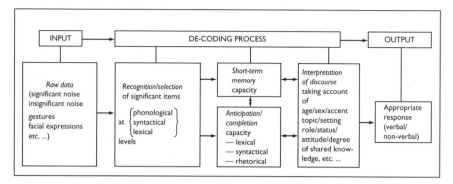

Figure 1.2 An information processing model of comprehension (Maley 1983: 17)

exploits what they already know about the speaker, their accent, the topic, the physical context, the background knowledge they share with the speaker, and so on. Eventually—though all this may take only milliseconds—the listener produces some form of appropriate output. All in all, this is a richer picture of listening comprehension than CT provided.

Although CT and IP approaches imply 'stages' of understanding, it is now recognized that when a spoken message is complex—and especially if we are having to respond to it in real time—we are only able to identify, interpret, and respond appropriately by using information from multiple sources simultaneously. This is known as **parallel distributed processing** and it forms part of the most recent version of the IP view of language processing: **connectionism**. The brain contains multiple series of networks of neurons (brain cells), each of which is connected thousands of times over to other networks. Our individual life experiences, and the meanings we associate with them, create the links among these neural networks. The frequency of an experience influences the 'strength' with which the neurons will fire (respond to particular input). An essential feature of the connectionist view of comprehension is that it is *probabilistic*; we work on the basis of *likely* meanings—'a reasonable interpretation' (Brown and Yule 1983a: 24)—rather than certainties.

Social Constructivism

The third theory—Social Constructivism—is radically different from CT and IP. Social Constructivism rejects the earlier mechanical and computational models, as being inappropriate to the ways in which human beings really communicate. Instead, it emphasizes the place of the individual in a social environment. The term 'Social Constructivism' covers a number of related approaches, such as sociocultural, sociocognitive, and ecological approaches. The one that has had the greatest influence so far on second language learning research and practice is the **Sociocultural Theory** (SCT) of the Soviet psychologist Lev Vygotsky (Vygotsky 1978). What these socially oriented approaches share is the fundamental principle that human cognition and learning are rooted in **interaction**. This was neatly summed up in the title of an early paper: 'Ask not what's inside your head, ask what your head's inside of' (Mace 1977). SCT claims that communicative interactions between human beings are not only central to understanding learning, but actually constitute the learning process itself:

> From an ecological perspective the learner is immersed in an environment full of potential meanings. These meanings become available gradually as the learner acts and interacts within and with this environment. Learning is not a … piecemeal migration of meanings to the inside of the learner's head, but rather the development of increasingly effective ways of dealing with the world and its meanings. (van Lier 2000: 246–7)

Social Constructivism regards human beings as participants in, and creators of, meaning; those meanings are achieved in the interactional space between us. Even in highly constrained contexts, such as those investigated in controlled experiments, conversational partners negotiate meanings and work towards a 'mutual cognitive environment' (Sperber and Wilson 1995: 61). In this sense, social constructivists take the view that the widespread use of computer metaphors such as 'input' and 'output' inevitably underestimates the active participation of the successful listener in interaction.

Summary

Communication Theory, Information Processing, and Social Constructivism should be seen as complementary theories, rather than as being mutually exclusive. Even the most limited of the three—CT—is adequate for describing certain limited listening tasks, such as taking down someone's telephone number or email address. But when we want to consider the full range of listening comprehension tasks, we find that successful listening processes are best explained by a combination of the theories so far available, as we will see in Chapters 3–5.

As I explained in the Preface, my own experiences as a second language listener have involved actual interaction with people, rather than virtual interaction with digital media. On the other hand, as a second language teacher I choose from a range of electronic devices to help develop my students' listening skills. The comments of the four listeners (the radio fan, the TV viewer, the iPod owner, and the laptop user) in this chapter underline the variety of media available today and also the range of listening roles that individuals can adopt, whether in their own language or another. Precisely what those roles involve, and how second language listeners can be guided to play them more effectively, is what we will be exploring in the rest of this book.

Suggestions for further reading

Lightbown P. and **N. Spada.** 2006. *How Languages are Learned.* 3rd edition. Oxford: Oxford University Press. Chapter 2, 'Explaining language learning', contains useful summaries of connectionism and Vygotsky's Sociocultural Theory.

Vandergrift, L. 2007. 'Recent developments in second and foreign language listening research.' *Language Teaching* 40: 191–210. A state-of-the-art review of the literature.

Discussion and study questions

1 The Listeners section gave us an insight into four different listening worlds. Which of them would you identify with most, in terms of your own listening experiences and preferences?

2 Michael Rost recently discussed the need for learners to encounter relevant and challenging listening input in the second language and wrote: 'We know that significant development in a second language requires a great quantity of input—certainly in the order of hundreds of hours per year. What is less clear is how the type and quality of input affects engagement and eventual acquisition' (Rost 2006: 49). Thinking back to your own experience as a second language listener, which types of listening input did you find most useful for improving (1) your listening ability, and (2) your knowledge of the language? When you have considered your own response to this question, ask your colleagues and your students what types of listening they think help them most.

3 Keep a listening diary for a couple of days, including a working day and a weekend. Make a note of the different sources of listening experience you encounter. If you use more than one language in that time, analyse whether the types of listening you do in those languages are different.

2 SPOKEN LANGUAGE

Introductory task

The extract below comes from a short talk recorded for a listening course in English for Academic Purposes. Do you think the person was speaking spontaneously, or using brief notes, or reading from a script? What evidence do you use in reaching your decision?

> When you have difficulty in identifying or remembering words and sentences, you obviously won't be able to follow the argument. But even those students who can do these things perfectly will have problems in following a quite straightforward argument. Why is this? I'll suggest three reasons here. Firstly, students don't always recognize the signals which tell the listener that certain points are important. Some of these signals will be quite different from those employed in writing. Secondly, some students try too hard to understand everything. When they come to a small but difficult point, they waste time trying to work it out, and so they may miss a more important point. Thirdly, students must concentrate very hard on taking notes and therefore may miss developments in the argument. But note-taking is a separate subject, which will be dealt with in a later talk. (James, Jordan, and Matthews 1979: 87)

Characteristics of spoken language

The fact that most people find it more difficult to listen to a second language than to read it is due in part to the features of natural speech, which we will be looking at in this chapter. However, it is important not to assume that spoken and written varieties are two completely distinct types of language. It is more accurate and more useful to think of speech and writing on a continuum—or, rather, several continua: from 'unplanned' to 'planned' (Ochs 1979); from 'oral' to 'literate' (Tannen 1982); from 'interactional' to 'transactional' (Brown and Yule 1983a); from 'involved' to 'detached' (Bygate 1998), and so on.

Feature	Examples
Grammar	
Chaining, rather than subordination	*so he goes into the pub—and he goes up to get his usual—but the barman's not there—and he waits for a bit—and in the end he decides to help himself to a lager...*
Ellipsis (omission)	*A: (Have you) Finished?* *B: (I will have in) Just a minute*
Shorter utterances, rather than long speaking turns	*A: How's the flat?* *B: It's fine, thanks.* *A: Did you move in over the weekend?* *B: Friday, actually*
Unfinished utterances, false starts	*I'd never... with all those little bones... I wouldn't normally buy kippers... anyway, hope they're ok*
Vocabulary	
General words rather than specific terms	*thing* *the whatsitsname* *stuff*
Fillers and hesitation markers	*well, um, like, uh...*
Deixis (referring to things in context)	*this one* *here* *her over there* *the bloke by the door*
Lexical chunks (prefabricated phrases)	*no sooner said than done* *in two minds* *never better*
Less explicit or vaguer language	*kind of* *a bit* *in a way* *or something like that*
Information	
Looser information structure	*see Shona with the white Peugeot—she is always in on a Tuesday—seems her brother Ian has broken his leg again—football mad, he is*
More redundancy and repetition	*The man with the hats—see the guy with the hats?—the old guy, not the young one—on the left—well he realizes the monkeys—or chimps, I suppose they are—the chimps have stolen his hats*

Table 2.1 Features of spoken English

The language in the extract from James, Jordan, and Matthews (1979) in the Introductory task suggests that the authors recorded a speaker who was reading from a prepared script, rather than someone talking from notes and to an audience. It seems to be planned ('I'll suggest three reasons here'), rather literate in its choice of formal lexis ('may miss developments in the argument', rather than 'may lose the thread' or 'may get lost', for instance), transactional (listing points for listeners to note and act upon), and detached (referring to the intended audience as 'students', rather than involving them as 'you', or the more empathetic 'we').

The same listening text may, of course, contain a mixture of different styles of spoken language. For instance, I have just watched a news programme on a natural disaster in South-East Asia; it consisted of a short opening report (scripted, written style) read aloud by the newsreader, followed by a live report (semi-scripted in note form, mixed style) from a BBC correspondent in the relevant location, and finally an interview between the correspondent and an eye-witness (unscripted, spoken style). Each of these components would occupy a different point in the multidimensional space created by the various continua mentioned above. Additional complexity arises from the fact that in some circumstances words may be carefully crafted to give the impression of spontaneous speech: a radio play, for instance, involves actors reading aloud a script written to sound as if it is *not* being read aloud.

Although speech and writing are clearly interrelated, there are clusters of features which we can expect to find more often in spoken language. These arise, according to Evelyn Hatch (Hatch 1992), from three principal parameters that differentiate the conditions under which speakers speak and writers write, namely 'planning', 'contextualization', and 'formality'. Speech will tend to be unplanned, tied to its immediate context, and informal. Among the characteristics of spoken language are those shown in Table 2.1, with invented examples.

Table 2.1 offers a sample of the commonest features of spoken English; it does not include the phonological characteristics of natural speech, which will be covered in Chapter 3. Among the features shown in the table, I will comment briefly on implicit reference and on redundancy.

Implicit reference

A marked feature of unplanned speech, particularly chat between friends, is the amount of information that is merely hinted at, rather than being made explicit. I recently heard a bus conversation in Edinburgh between an elderly woman and a younger woman who had obviously not seen each other for some time and were interested in catching up on each other's lives. The exchange between them went something like this:

OLDER WOMAN	What about wee Jackie? Is it still sort of on or sort of off?
YOUNGER WOMAN	Well, you *ken* (= know) our Jackie. With her it's never really on and it's never really off, if you get my drift.
OLDER WOMAN	*Och, aye,* (= Oh, yes) I get your drift fine.

My impression was that the younger woman deliberately chose the expression 'if you get my drift' (in the sense of 'if you understand what I am implying') because in this relatively public setting she did not want, and did not *need*, to go into further detail as to what the topic ('it') was that they were talking about. I thought it could have been an engagement, a wedding, or a decision to go to university, but of course I cannot be sure.

Indirect reference and ellipsis are typical of talk between family, friends, and close colleagues. In an interesting piece of research, my University of Edinburgh colleague Joan Cutting recorded, over several months, the coffee room conversations among a group of students taking a Master's course at Edinburgh (Cutting 2000). She found that over time the students used progressively more indirect and implicit expressions; clearly, the more we know about each other, the more knowledge we share and the less we need to refer to it directly.

Redundancy

However, for the language learner, the picture is not all bleak: spontaneous spoken language offers the listener various compensatory features, of which perhaps the most helpful are redundancy and non-verbal communication. Speakers repeat and rephrase more than writers do, which helps the listener to process the intended meaning of what is being said by allowing more time to take in what we are hearing. But second language listeners may need to be guided to take advantage of this redundancy by being shown that not every new utterance necessarily contains new information and by being trained to listen out for the discourse markers that signal redundancy, such as 'in other words'.

The overall effect of the greater redundancy of speech, combined with the lower levels of grammatical subordination, is to provide the listener with information that is much less dense than is usual in written language. 'We must assume that the density of information packaging in spoken language is appropriate for the listener to process comfortably' (Brown and Yule 1983b: 18). More recently, Scott Thornbury and Diana Slade commented on the relative advantages of lower lexical density for listeners:

> Lower lexical density is partly a consequence of production pressure. But the more thinly spread occurrence of propositional content, as represented in lexical words, also helps to make spoken language easier to process by listeners, who, like speakers, are also having to work under the constraints of real-time processing. (Thornbury and Slade 2006:13)

That claim is borne out by the findings of research studies: listeners to language texts that are closer to the spoken end of the speech/writing continuum understand more than listeners working with texts closer to the written end. Elana Shohamy of Tel Aviv University and Ofra Inbar of Beit Berle Teachers' College found that Hebrew-speaking learners of English who listened to a short monologue (extemporized from written notes) achieved higher comprehension scores than other students who heard a news broadcast (scripted monologue) on the same topic (Shohamy and Inbar 1991). Similarly, in a study involving American students of Russian at Georgetown University, Irene Thompson reported that conversations lead to better comprehension scores than expository written passages (Thompson 1993).

Non-verbal communication

The second way in which speech allows the listener to benefit from additional information is the fact it is accompanied, at least in face-to-face interaction, by two types of non-verbal and visual clues to meaning.

Firstly, speakers have at their disposal a wide range of expressive devices, which contribute to the listener's grasp of what they are meant to understand (Harmer 2001). These include changes in pitch and volume, and the placement of stress to highlight specific words, and they also extend to non-linguistic cues, such as facial expressions and body language. Some of these devices have equivalents in the written language—such as the use of a different font or underlining to indicate the word that would be stressed in speech—but in general the listener is able to exploit a greater variety of expressive cues than are available to the reader.

Secondly, the listener can exploit the visual information the speaker provides. The analysis by Philip Riley, of CRAPEL (Centre de Recherches et d'Applications Pédagogiques en Langues) at the University of Nancy II, of the potential wealth of such information remains, even after nearly three decades, one of the best discussions of the role of the visual in listening comprehension (Riley 1981). Writing at a time when video materials were just beginning to make their mark in language teaching, Philip Riley wrote that the visual aspects of communication 'are not to be despised; true, they lack the semantic referential precision of the verbal component, but in pragmatic and relational terms they are generally far more important' (Riley 1981: 145). He teased out a number of basic functions of visual information, among them the five listed below:

Deictic—Pointing to nearby objects
Interactional—Signals of turn taking, such as adjustments of body position
Modal—Expressing the speaker's commitment to what they are saying, for example, mouth turned down at the corners and eyebrows raised, to indicate one is relaying someone else's opinion or decision

Indexical—Indicators of 'self'; for example, posture, clothes
Linguistic—Replacing certain verbal expressions, such as beckoning instead of 'come here'.

Some of these visual cues, such as head-scratching, appear to be universal; others may be culture-specific, or may have a universal primary meaning and secondary meanings that are culture-specific. For example, it took me some time to realize that Brazilians may use finger clicks to mean 'a long time ago', as well as to attract someone's attention, while in Britain some people also use finger clicking to indicate that we are trying to remember something. A fully competent second language user should be able to integrate these signals with the spoken message—a point made recently by Tony Harris, in a paper whose title, 'Listening with your eyes', echoes Philip Riley's 'L'oeuil écoute' (Harris 2003). Therefore, although we conventionally talk of the development of 'listening' skills, we must not lose sight of the key role played by non-verbal expression in support of the spoken word, especially in the case of a second language.

Learners' perceptions of spoken language

Speed

The fact that the speech that learners encounter outside the language classroom is normally temporary (unless recorded) and may require an immediate response means that the overwhelming impression of listening to another language is one of speed, and a lack of control over the speaker. Speed is certainly the source of difficulty most often mentioned by my own EFL students when we discuss the relative problems of listening and reading. Michael Rost has discussed the same perception among his students of English in Japan and in the USA (Rost 2002); and Suzanne Graham reported similar comments in her recent survey of secondary school students learning French in England (Graham 2006).

One might make the commonsense assumption that as **speech rate** (measured as the number of words or syllables a speaker utters per minute) increases, the level of comprehension falls, but actually the evidence on the effect of speech rate on second language comprehension is rather mixed. Ken Kelch, of the University of Hawaii, measured intermediate-level ESL students' scores on four versions of a dictation text:

1 unmodified
2 spoken slowly
3 modified in ways typical of **foreigner talk**
4 Version 3 delivered at a slowed rate

(Kelch 1985: 84).

The students' answers were marked in two ways: one focusing on form and the other on meaning. On both measures, a slowed speech rate assisted comprehension. However, version 4, which combined both types of modification, increased the listeners' scores only when assessed for meaning, rather than form. Ken Kelch speculated that this difference might be linked to the distinction between messages that are cognitively, rather than linguistically, simpler. The grammatical modifications of Versions 3 and 4 may have made them cognitively more accessible, which helped listeners to understand them better but made exact recall of form more difficult.

Janet Anderson-Hsieh and Kenneth Koehler, working at Iowa State University, found that passages delivered at slow rates by both native and non-native speakers of English were significantly easier to understand for second language listeners than the same texts read at higher speeds (Anderson-Hsieh and Koehler 1988). Roger Griffiths, who was one of the leading researchers in this particular area, also found that speech faster than 200 words per minute (w.p.m.) was difficult for lower-intermediate EFL learners to understand (Griffiths 1990). However, there was no significant difference for these learners between speech delivered at a slow rate (100 w.p.m.) and that delivered at an average rate (150 w.p.m.).

One of the reasons for this mixed picture is that different researchers have used different methods. Speech can be slowed mechanically (by speech compression) or by conscious, but variable, efforts on the part of the speaker. Texts may be unplanned or semi-scripted or fully scripted. The listening tasks set in different research studies have also varied. Paul King and Ralph Behnke investigated the possible interaction between speech rate and listening task type in a study of native English speakers at Texas Christian University, Fort Worth, using three types of task: comprehensive listening—understanding and remembering for future use; interpretive listening—inferring or detecting implied meaning; and short-term listening—receiving, processing, and remembering for a limited period (King and Behnke 1989). They found that as speech rates increased, the scores on comprehensive listening scores fell, while those for interpretive and short-term listening were not affected.

A further refinement of our knowledge of how speech rate affects second language listening has come with the finding that it is speakers' patterns of stress and rhythm that affect listening difficulty, rather than the raw measure of syllables or words per minute. In a classroom study conducted with advanced ESL learners at Heriot-Watt University in Edinburgh and using a recorded television interview with Margaret Thatcher, Robert Vanderplank found that the group of learners perceived Mrs Thatcher's style of speaking to be both slow and rapid (Vanderplank 1993). In answer to his own question—'How can the lady speak slowly yet quickly?'—he argued that the listeners' perceptions reflected Mrs Thatcher's particular **pacing** and **spacing**. Pacing means the tempo at which stressed words are spoken (for example, 50 per minute); spacing refers to the proportion of stressed words in the total number of words (for example, 1 to 4). What made her spoken English distinctive and difficult for listeners—not only second language listeners!—was its combination of a higher number of syllables stressed for emphasis, and bursts of relatively rapid utterances with pauses between them.

In a study at the École Supérieure de Commerce in Troyes, France, which compared groups of learners of English at different levels (advanced French learners and intermediate Japanese learners), Brett Berquist investigated differences in the level of comprehension of three types of spoken text: normal speed, slowed speech, and normal-speed speech into which pauses had been inserted (Berquist 1994). He found that the advanced learners did best on the third type of text, but the same was not true of the intermediate learners. This suggested that when speakers make short pauses in their speech, it provides more proficient listeners with additional 'space' to process or review what they have just heard and that pausing may be more helpful than simply speaking slower.

Accent

Research into the effect of accent on the comprehension of English by second language learners has tended to be associated with university contexts, where international students who attend lectures in English have reported that lecturers' accents represent an obstacle to understanding—for example, in Singapore (Kennedy 1978), Hawaii (Richards 1983; Bilbow 1989), and the University of Georgetown (Mason 1994). But, as far as I am aware, there is no research evidence that specific accents of English—native or non-native—are *inherently* more difficult than others for second language listeners to understand. It seems more likely that accents, and the value judgements they give rise to, illustrate the general case that what is *unfamiliar* requires greater attention for human beings to make sense of it. As second language listeners become more familiar with an individual speaker with a particular accent, they gradually have less difficulty in understanding it. However, the same may not be true of native listeners, at least in Britain: there is evidence, for example, that British attitudes to certain accents colour perceptions of the speaker's sincerity or authority (Coupland and Bishop 2007).

The reverse is also true: there is no evidence that any particular non-native accents are intrinsically more problematic for native English listeners than any other. A foreign speaker may have, or may adopt, a highly marked accent without causing their listeners serious difficulties; it depends how familiar the listener is with that particular variety of English. In Britain, the television presenter Antoine de Caunes was able to exaggerate his French accent for comic effect without reducing his comprehensibility, precisely because the French accent is probably the most familiar to British viewers. Empirical evidence of the power of familiarity comes from a study at the University of Michigan by Susan Gass and Evangeline Marlos Varonis, who examined American native speakers' comprehension of Japanese and Arabic learners of English (Gass and Varonis 1984). The native speakers—some students, others ESL teachers—were asked to transcribe English sentences read aloud by the two groups of learners. In all cases, the ESL teachers made fewer errors than the native students, indicating that familiarity was the key. 'Familiarity takes on a broad perspective, involving not only immediate factors such as pronunciation, but also background information such as real-world expectations' (Gass and Varonis 1984: 82).

Representing spoken language: transcripts

So far I have used conventional spelling and punctuation in the examples of spoken language I have quoted, but in later chapters I will in some cases be using a different transcription system. It is essential always to keep in mind that a transcript and the speech it represents are not the same thing. The original is a richer, contextualized communicative event. The transcript will be only as accurate a version of what the speaker said, and how they said it, as is needed by the person doing the transcribing. To create a precise replica of original speech would require information not simply on the sounds made by the speaker—'the segmental record' (Brown and Yule 1983b: 10)—but also of their intonation and rhythm, in the sort of detail that Robert Vanderplank's research suggests is important.

A further issue arises in cases of interaction recalled and transcribed by second language learners, namely that what they write in the transcript may not be what was said but what they *understood* to have been said. This was the case in the 'cup' incident in the Introductory task in Chapter 1. What I presented there was a translation of what I thought I had heard, rather than what had actually been said in the original Portuguese. Table 2.2 provides a fuller version, separating out what was said, what I understood, and what I began to have doubts about.

My confusion arose from the fact that I had not realized that I was on the wrong track from the very beginning. When the girl used *mexerica*, I did not realize it was a word I did not know; it is Portuguese for 'tangerine'. I understood it as 'my cup' and had no idea why the girl should be asking for her cup in our house. The mother was embarrassed, and the other people laughed, because her daughter had asked for food in someone else's house, which would be regarded as rude—even for a five-year-old, apparently—and a reflection on parental upbringing.

What was said/done	What I understood	What I wondered
tem uma mexerica, tem?	*tem a minha xirica, tem?* (= do you have my cup?)	but 'cup' is *xícara*
o, vou morrer de vergonha!	*o, vou morrer de vergonha!* (= oh, I'll die of embarrassment!)	why should she be embarrassed?
Everyone laughs, except me		why the laughter? 1 is a *xirica* a trainer cup for toddlers? 2 is *xirica* a child's linguistic error?
vamos escolher uma	*vamos escolher uma* (= let's go and choose one)	choose one <u>what</u>?
They come back into the room. The little girl is carrying a tangerine on a plate. Everyone laughs.		I still don't get it, but I join in as well. What's so funny?

Table 2.2 Confusion of a second language listener

The right-hand column represents what I recalled of my efforts to make sense of it all, eventually joining in the laughter without knowing what was funny. I assume this sort of mishearing and consequent confusion is typical of second language listening, but normally goes unseen when the listener does what I did and pretends to have understood.

In the later chapters of this book, when I present a transcript of my classroom or other data, I use an adapted version of the system used by Gillian Brown and colleagues (Brown and Yule 1983a and 1983b; Brown, Anderson, Shillcock, and Yule 1984). It shows utterances separated by pauses (using the symbols +, ++, or +++ to indicate relative length), rather than presenting them as written sentences with a capital letter at the start and a full stop at the end. In some cases, I use initial letters to represent the speakers; in others, I use pseudonyms. When I use transcripts from other publications, I will present them in the form adopted by the author(s).

Summary

Spoken language contains different characteristics from most forms of written language. Some of those features, such as increased ellipsis and indirect reference, tend to make speech more difficult for second language listeners to follow. By way of compensation, spoken language also tends to display features that make comprehension easier—higher levels of redundancy and pausing between idea chunks. Language teachers need to make learners aware of the typical patterns of speech they are likely to encounter and to help them to take advantage of the potentially helpful cues that speakers provide. The more we realize the 'reduced' nature of spoken language, the more we appreciate the mental effort that listeners need to put in to make sense. Whilst the clear information structure and unhesitant delivery of a pedagogic script like the one in the Introductory task will tend to make listening comprehension easier than it would be with unplanned speech, second language listening instruction at all levels should provide a broad mix of spoken **genres**, so that learners get used to the looser structure and more elliptical nature of unplanned speech. Finally, we need to be aware of the key role played by visual and non-verbal information in the way we interpret what a speaker says, and try, whenever possible, to base our second language listening activities on video rather than audio materials.

Suggestions for further reading

Studies in Second Language Acquisition. 2008. Special issue (30/2) 'Gesture and SLA: Towards an Integrated Approach.' A collection highlighting the intimate relationship between the visual and spoken components of second language speech.

Thornbury, S. and **D. Slade.** 2006. *Conversation: From Description to Pedagogy*. Cambridge: Cambridge University Press.

Discussion and study questions

1 Record yourself (or someone else) giving instructions for making something—for example, a recipe, or telling a story or joke. Do not rehearse it before you start the recording. Then transcribe the speaker's words as exactly as you can, using plus symbols (+, ++, or +++) to show the relative length of pauses. What difficulties, if any, do you encounter in making the transcript? Which of the features of spoken English from Table 2.1 can you observe in the performance?

2 'Introspective reports can be useful to both researchers and teachers because they allow us to understand some of the cognitive constraints that are usually invisible to an outside observer... Moreover, by providing opportunities for learners to report in their own words, we might gain some insights into their understanding of and attitude towards some of these difficulties' (Goh 2000: 3). Next time you are teaching a listening class, ask the students to spend a few minutes writing down—in their first

language, if you are familiar with it—what they found difficult in listening to or watching the material they listened to, and how they tried to resolve the problem(s). Take in and analyse their self-reports. What do the students' comments suggest are common problems? What are your possible actions as their listening teacher?

3 Record a short extract from a television drama, film, or advertisement. Use the soundtrack only as listening material in class, or play the recording with the screen turned to black. How much of the meaning of the text was obscured by the learners not seeing the visual cues?

PART TWO

Listening processes

3 RECOGNITION

Introductory task

My radio is normally set to come on at 7.25 in the morning. One day I woke up and heard the final part of an interview. What I remember hearing was:

INTERVIEWER how do you rate Bob?
EXPERT oh he's got to be the greatest six-bender ever
INTERVIEWER and where do you see him going from here?
EXPERT well actually he's already got one girlfriend lined up for tomorrow and another one for Friday
INTERVIEWER sounds like Ballyregan Bob could soon be breaking world records of a rather different sort + thanks very much for coming on this morning
EXPERT my pleasure Gary

Are there any parts of the text that you think I must have *mis*heard?

Levelt's model of spoken language use

The successful production and understanding of speech requires the skilled coordination of immensely complex processes. The best-known model of

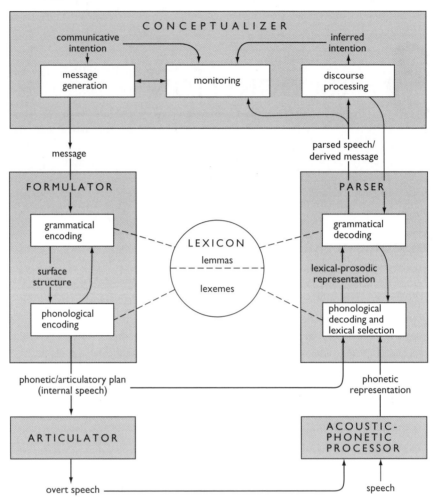

Figure 3.1 A model of spoken communication (Levelt 1993: 2)

these processes is the one developed by the Dutch psychologist Willem Levelt, in which speaking and listening are represented as mirror images of each other (Levelt 1993). Speaking involves three components: a Conceptualizer, which decides what you want to say; a Formulator, which works out how to say it; and an Articulator, which produces it. For our purposes I will be focusing on the components of the listening process: an Acoustic-Phonetic Processor, a Parser, and the Conceptualizer.

For a listener to understand what a speaker says, their Acoustic-Phonetic Processor must first analyse the speech signal and produce a phonetic representation. This is not always straightforward, even in our own language, because the acoustic shape of a word depends on its linguistic context, its stress and intonation, the speaker's sex, dialect and speed of speaking, the presence of background noise, and so on. But the Acoustic-Phonetic

Processor produces as precise a representation as possible of what the speaker has said, and passes it on to the Parser.

The Parser is responsible for **phonological decoding** and **lexical selection**. First, it matches the phonetic representation with the phonological template for the language in question. The major problem in listening to connected speech is **lexical segmentation**—recognizing where one word ends and the next one begins. Natural speech does not usually provide helpful gaps between words (equivalent to the spaces in written text) and languages vary in the degree of help they offer in this segmentation process; in Finnish, for example, words are normally pronounced with main stress on their first syllable, which makes it easier to identify where the preceding word ends. Once the Parser has chunked a string of sounds as a potential word, it matches it against the mental lexicon, where it is able to access the grammatical and semantic information associated with that word, and to test whether the word identified seems plausible.

The final component in the model, the Conceptualizer, enables the listener to grasp the speaker's intended meaning—what Willem Levelt calls 'discourse processing'. Having established what the speaker has said, the Conceptualizer searches for reasons why the speaker has said what they have said, exploiting the listener's relevant background knowledge and their sociocultural experience of discourse.

I am going to use a concrete example, from Finnish, of how Levelt's model would work. (I have chosen Finnish because it is a potentially listener-friendly language in two respects: in addition to the regular first-syllable stress, there is a close relationship between the way Finnish words are pronounced and spelt.) Imagine you are in Helsinki and have just got out of your car, when a woman in a uniform comes up and says something to you which your Acoustic/ Phonetic Processor analyses as *anteeksipysäköintionkiellettytässä*. Since you know that stress is normally on the first syllable, your Parser segments the utterance into five words, *anteeksi pysäköinti on kielletty tässä*. A search of your limited mental lexicon of Finnish allows you to recognize three of those words: *anteeksi* is 'excuse me'; *on* is the present tense of the verb 'to be'; and *tässä* means 'here'. Your Conceptualizer searches for possible reasons why the woman is telling you that '(*pysäköinti*) is (*kielletty*) here', and the fact that she is smiling and pointing at a sign on a post which reads *Pysäköinti kielletty* is enough for you to recognize the utterance as a reminder, from this particularly polite traffic warden, that this is a no-parking area and you need to move your car somewhere else.

Willem Levelt emphasizes that the components in his model of spoken language do not necessarily work one after the other, in stages. Understanding real-time speech makes such demands on listeners that we can only succeed by processing different elements of a message at the same time, in parallel, as we saw in Chapter 1. This parallel processing is only feasible because most components are fully automatic—at least, in our first language. But under some circumstances what is normally automatic recognition breaks down. Two years ago I was listening to the radio commentary on a rugby match between England and France, in which one of the French players had the surname Traille. The English commentator pronounced the name with a southern English approximant *r*, as opposed to a French uvular *r*, and as a result the name sounded exactly the same as the English word 'try'. Since 'try' is also a technical term in rugby—referring to the equivalent of a touch-down in American football—it meant that every time I heard the sound string /trai/, I had to decide whether the commentator was naming the player or describing a score.

Levelt's model was originally designed to describe first language communication, and at an abstract and general level; he did not analyse the skills that go to make up listening. When it comes to a second language, listeners need to apply and coordinate a large number of micro-skills, which they use automatically in their first language—perhaps as many as 33 micro-skills for conversation and 18 for listening to lectures (Richards 1983). To make the picture simpler and more manageable, Michael Rost has proposed that, for practical purposes of second language classroom instruction, it makes sense to think in terms of five clusters of skills, as shown in Table 3.1.

The representation of listening skills in terms of the five skill clusters is broadly similar to John Anderson's IP model of comprehension, which we looked at in Chapter 1: Perception (cluster 1 in Table 3.1), Parsing (clusters 2–4), and Utilization (cluster 5). In this chapter and in Chapters 4 and 5, I will be discussing research into those three elements of listening comprehension, using the terms 'recognition', 'interpretation', and 'participation'.

Lexical segmentation: how to wreck a nice beach

As we try to identify words in the stream of second language speech, the **prosody** (stress, rhythm, and intonation) of our first language exerts a very powerful influence on the recognition process. In the first three or four years of our lives the first language's characteristic patterning fixes in our minds a sort of 'metrical template', which enables us to recognize what we hear. English is predominantly trochaic (strong syllable followed by weak), while French is iambic (weak syllable followed by strong). Listeners exploit these characteristics to identify words in spontaneous speech, which typically offers few cues to signal word boundaries. For example, English and Dutch speakers tend to segment speech at the onset of strong syllables, while French speakers do the same after what they perceive to be the final syllable

Enabling skills

Perception

1 Recognizing prominence within utterances, including
   - discriminating sounds in words, esp. phonemic contrasts
   - discriminating strong and weak forms, phonetic change at word boundaries
   - identifying use of stress and pitch (information units, emphasis, etc.).

Interpretation

2 Formulating content sense of an utterance, including
   - deducing the meaning of unfamiliar words
   - inferring implicit information
   - inferring links between propositions.

3 Formulating a conceptual framework linking utterances, including
   - recognizing discourse markers (introducing a new idea, clarifying, and contrasting)
   - constructing a theme over a stretch of discourse
   - predicting content
   - identifying elements that help you to form an overall schema
   - maintaining and updating the context.

4 Interpreting (possible) speaker intentions, including
   - identifying an 'interpersonal frame' speaker-to-hearer
   - monitoring changes in prosody and establishing (in)consistencies
   - noting contradictions, inadequate information, ambiguities
   - differentiating between fact and opinion.

Enacting skills

Participation

5 Making an appropriate response (based on 1–4 above), including
   - identifying which points need to be clarified by the speaker
   - providing appropriate feedback to the speaker
   - selecting relevant points to pick up or comment on.

Table 3.1 Enabling skills and enacting skills in listening (adapted from Rost 1990: 152–3)

of a rhythmic group (Cutler, Dahan, and van Donselaar 1997). It is only at relatively advanced levels of proficiency in a second language that we are able to inhibit our misapplication of our native language strategies (Delabatie and Bradley 1995; Cutler 2000).

There is evidence that in English native listeners use main syllable stress as the *primary* means of identifying words in speech when listening to fellow native speakers (Cutler 2000). A recent study carried out at La Trobe University by Beth Zielinski found that English native speakers also applied the same stress-based segmentation strategy when listening to second language speakers (Zielinski 2008). In her experiment three Australian, native English speakers with no particular experience of native–non-native interaction were asked to transcribe extracts from the conversational spoken English of three second language speakers from Korean, Mandarin, and Vietnamese backgrounds who had TOEFL scores of 580 or more. The focus of the study was on 'sites of reduced intelligibility', or parts of the speakers' utterances where one or more of the listeners failed, or found it difficult, to identify what the speaker intended to say.

Beth Zielinski found that the listeners relied heavily and consistently on the speaker's placement of syllable stress and on their production of the consonants and vowels in strongly stressed syllables. They encountered particular difficulty when both the syllable-initial consonant and the vowel were pronounced in a non-standard way. One such case of non-standard segments and misplaced stress occurred in the speech of the Korean speaker, who changed both /b/ and /f/ to /p/ in the word 'before' and placed the main stress on the first syllable, as /ˈpiːpoː/ As a result, all three listeners transcribed the word as 'people'. The study shows that these listeners made no apparent **adjustments** to their native speech processing strategies when listening to people they knew were second language users of English— despite realizing they were encountering difficulty in understanding the recordings.

There is also evidence that the role played by syllable stress in a listener's first language influences the way they process stress in the second language. In Spanish, for example, similar words may be differentiated solely by their stress pattern, as they are in English: two different tense forms of the verb *pasar* are marked as *pasaran* (with second syllable stress) and *pasarán* (with third syllable stress). Spanish listeners have been shown to be more skilled at discriminating stress placement in nonsense strings than French listeners, whose language does not exploit stress phonologically in that way (Dupoux, Pallier, Sebastian, and Mehler 1997).

Most languages present the listener with difficulties in the form of acoustic blurring of lexical boundaries in natural speech. Certainly, in English the shape of words in connected speech is strongly affected by the sounds that precede and follow them: 'in fast speech words do not occur one after the other like a line of bricks' (Cauldwell 1996: 522). We are not short of helpful descriptions of typical patterns of simplification in natural spoken English. Gillian Brown devoted nearly 30 pages of her classic *Listening to Spoken English* (Brown 1977) to explaining the processes of assimilation (the merging of phonemes at word boundaries, as in the production of /g/

for /d/ in /ˈɑməgˈkɑ/ in 'armoured car') and of elision (the omission of sounds, as in /əzknˈfjuzəzˈevə/ for 'as confused as ever'). An earlier guide for second language learners of English (Windsor Lewis 1969) provided 11 pages of information about the weak forms of vowels that can make it difficult for learners to recognize words that are, in fact, part of their vocabulary:

THE 7 ATTRIBUTES:	a – an – the – some – Saint – our – his
THE 5 PERSONAL PRONOUNS:	he – him – her – us – them
THE 5 CONJUNCTIONS:	and – but – as – than – that
THE 5 PREPOSITIONS:	at – for – from – of – to
THE 14 VERBAL FINITES:	do – does – am – is – are – was – shall – will – can – must – have – has – had – would

The fact that most of those 36 words are among the commonest in spoken English adds to the second language listener's difficulty in segmenting running speech. In this respect, English presents greater problems than languages such as Hungarian and Italian, where there is a closer relationship between the spoken and written word. English is also one of the many languages with multi-syllable words, which may contain phonetically identical or near-identical shorter 'words' embedded within them, such as 'wreck', 'reckon', and 'eyes' within the word 'recognize'—which is why 'How to recognize speech' may be heard as 'How to wreck a nice beach'. It has been said that around 85 per cent of polysyllabic English words contain embedded words (Cutler 1997), adding to the potential difficulties faced by the second language listener.

Vocabulary

Compared with the amount of research into the relationship between vocabulary knowledge and reading ability in a second language, there has been relatively little into the links between vocabulary and listening. To language teachers this may seem odd. After all, a common classroom technique for preparing a group of learners for a listening task is to select the words we think they are unlikely to know and to 'pre-teach' them those words. We also know from our own daily experience that hearing an unfamiliar word can delay or impede understanding. For example, in the case of the radio interview in the Introductory task to this chapter, I was convinced that the interviewee had used the word 'six-bender', although I had never heard it before. I then remembered that Ballyregan Bob was the name of a champion greyhound at the time, so I was able to work out that a 'six-bender' must be a dog that specializes in races involving three laps (or six bends) of the oval track used for greyhound racing. Having just broken the world record for the longest sequence of consecutive victories, Bob was being retired to stud— hence the reference to the two 'girlfriends'.

One of the earliest studies of the relationship between vocabulary level and listening was conducted by Peter Kelly at the University of Namur (Kelly 1991), who compared the transcription errors made by an advanced user of English (a French EFL teacher) with those made by a group of French undergraduates at intermediate level. He found that just under two-thirds of all the errors where there was evidence of severely impaired comprehension were lexical errors, and concluded that 'lexical ignorance is by far the most frequent cause of lack of comprehension' (Kelly 1991: 147). His proposed remedy for learners' limited vocabulary was a fairly obvious one: to expand their second language lexis—in particular, teaching and practising the spoken form of words.

Research by Steven Ross shed further light on the role of word identification in the comprehension process of second language listeners with limited proficiency (Ross 1997). He investigated how learners construct and modify **mental models**—or fail to modify them—in the light of incoming information. The subjects in his study were Japanese learners of English at university in Japan. They were asked to match icons (for example, of a train or plane) with a recorded message (for example, a sentence describing the problems of a rail journey), and then to introspect in Japanese about how they decided which icon to choose. By analysing their introspective recall of what went through their mind, Steven Ross identified eight 'processing stages', ranging from the more basic (and unsuccessful) to the more complex and effective:

1 noise—no response
2 distraction—process overload
3 syllable restructuring—mishearing
4 syllable identification
5 key word association
6 linking with more than one key word
7 recognition of phrases
8 recognition of whole utterances.

(Ross 1997: 222–6)

For the weaker listeners, Stage 5—key word association—was the commonest level of processing. They produced an initial mental model based on a key word and kept to it, without searching for confirming cues, while the more proficient listeners also frequently operated at Stage 5 but had sufficient capacity to hold the key word in short-term memory while they searched for support in the message. The results of this experiment supported the findings of earlier research by Gabriele Kasper, then of the University of Aarhus, who found that lower-level German learners of English tended to form a mental model of what they were hearing and were then reluctant to abandon it, even when what they heard subsequently clearly contradicted it (Kasper

1984). The second language listener's relative reluctance to replace an existing hypothesis with one that matches more recent information has again been confirmed by John Field's recent work on lexical segmentation, in a study which compared the listening processes of first and second language users of English (Field 2008).

Overall, it would seem reasonable to assume that knowledge of vocabulary plays a significant role in second language comprehension, but until recently that assumption was based on research into second language reading. The first researcher to test the assumption in listening comprehension was Frances Mecartty, who investigated the relationship between the lexical and grammatical proficiency and listening performance of 154 English-speaking second-year, non-major students of Spanish at the University of Denver. She found that, while their grammatical knowledge was not a significant factor in their listening comprehension scores, their knowledge of Spanish vocabulary accounted for around 15 per cent of listening success. Frances Mecartty concluded that 'lexical knowledge appears to be more crucial to reading than it is to listening' (Mecartty 2000: 340)—which should perhaps be understood as meaning that lexical knowledge is more easily accessed in reading, where the text is visible, than in listening, where the learner in a sense has to recreate the text.

Larry Vandergrift of the University of Ottawa extended this area of research to examine the possible relationship between second language proficiency, second language listening, and first language listening ability (Vandergrift 2006). The learners in his study were 75 English-speaking, Canadian secondary school pupils studying French as a second language. They were given similar tests of their English and French listening comprehension, based on short dialogues. Analysis of their scores showed that both second language proficiency and listening ability contribute to second language listening, but to different degrees, with second language proficiency having the greater influence. When the pupils' scores were broken down into type of comprehension (literal and inferential), it emerged that second language proficiency was a more important factor in success in literal comprehension. Larry Vandergrift argues that lexical knowledge is essential for literal questions: 'students cannot draw on world knowledge as much when it comes to answering questions concerning details that require knowledge of specific L2 words' (Vandergrift 2006: 14). Both Frances Mecartty and Larry Vandergrift emphasize that, given the evidence of a strong effect of vocabulary in second language listening, it is essential that instruction in vocabulary development with the aim of helping learners' listening should include and highlight practice in aural lexical recognition of the natural form(s) of words in connected speech—the word in the ear, rather than the word on the page.

Syntax

Although second language learners more often ascribe their listening problems to lack of vocabulary, it was the role of syntax in comprehension that
received more attention from researchers in the 1960s and 1970s, particularly
under the influence of Noam Chomsky's work in transformational and gen-
erative grammar. They were interested in the relative difficulty of understanding
different syntactic structures, and the ways in which their comprehension
might play out differently for first and second language listeners. For example,
Vivian Cook of the University of Essex compared the difficulties experienced
by young first language listeners and adult second language learners when
they encountered pairs of sentences such as those below:

1 The dog is easy to bite
2 The dog is eager to bite

The results of his research (Cook 1973) suggested that in sentences like the
first one, where the noun in normal subject position is not the agent but the
object of the action, both the young native listeners and the second language
listeners appeared to progress through a stage of development in which they
tended to misinterpret 'the dog' as the agent. More advanced second language learners and older first language listeners correctly distinguished the
role of the dog in the two sentences.

In the 1980s attention moved to studying how listeners coped with more
natural spoken texts. Bernd Voss of the University of Bielefeld compared
word recognition in first and second language of a group of German undergraduate students, who had studied English for about ten years (Voss 1984).
He asked them to produce a word-for-word transcription of two recordings of natural conversation, one in English and the other in German. He
set no time limit and allowed the students to replay the recording as many
times as they liked. Bernd Voss chose English and German recordings from
interviews containing spontaneous speech with natural characteristics such
as hesitations, filled pauses, and self-corrections. The topics, though, were
different in the two languages: the English recording was about youth work,
which could be considered reasonably accessible to the undergraduates; the
German text featured an absurdist artist discussing his plans to sell his suit
and its surrounding personal space to an art gallery. These topics were chosen
to balance the listeners' relative ease with the *form* of the German text against
the likely unfamiliarity of its *content*, and vice versa for the English text.

The results of the transcribing experiment showed a striking degree of simi-
larity in the students' performances in German and English. The number,
type, and distribution of recognition errors was very much the same for both
first and second language listening. However, there was an important issue
of level: these undergraduates had been learning English for ten years or so
and were majoring in the language at university, so one can assume that they

had a relatively advanced level of second language proficiency. So there could have been a circular effect at work: the reason for the striking similarities between these listeners' performances in first and second languages was that they had reached a relatively native-like level in English. Bernd Voss's study left open the important question of how the less proficient second language listener copes with word recognition problems.

For evidence of how Levelt's Parser might work in listening at different levels of second language proficiency, we can turn to a study by Linda Conrad of Michigan State University (Conrad 1985). It drew on findings from second language reading research that less proficient readers depend more on syntactic clues and less on semantic ones than readers at higher levels, so that their processing is somehow 'short-circuited' when facing a demanding second language text (Clarke 1979). Linda Conrad's subjects were six groups of university students: two groups of native English users, two groups of advanced second language listeners, and two groups at intermediate level. Each of the three subject levels were divided into a Listening group and a Non-listening group. The Listening groups heard a recorded lecture in English and then completed a cloze reading test based on the lecture transcript. The Non-listeners did the cloze test without hearing the lecture. The findings confirmed the hypotheses from the reading research: the native English listeners relied mainly on semantic clues, while the second language listeners tended to rely on syntactic clues. Linda Conrad also established an effect of proficiency level: within the second language listeners, those at intermediate level made most use of immediate, local syntactic context and least use of global meaning in the text.

In recent years there has been very little research into the influence of syntax on second language listening. Such studies as there have been suggest that syntax has much less effect than vocabulary; earlier I cited the study by Frances Mecartty, which found no measurable effect for syntax (Mecartty 2000). However, a recent paper by Gillian Brown of the University of Cambridge, which reviews experimental research in the first language comprehension of English and French, explored the differences in the way native users process syntactic forms in a printed or spoken text, as demonstrated by their recall of those texts (Brown 2008). In particular, Gillian Brown focused on listeners' processing of forms under stressful conditions, such as having to respond in real time to spoken instructions that are unclear or contradict other information available. She found some evidence of a syntactic 'hierarchy', with listeners tending to recall nouns more often than verbs, and verbs more often than adjectives and adverbs. It seems that nouns are most salient for the listener when they occur as subject or object of a verb, rather than in a prepositional phrase. Nouns in subject or object position appear to act as anchors for the reader's or listener's understanding and recall of a text. So syntax may well affect native listeners' comprehension in a more fundamental way, rather than through the individual's grammatical knowledge. This appears likely also to apply to second language listeners, though that issue remains to be investigated.

Summary

Research into listeners' ability to decode second language speech—to recognize what is being said—have highlighted the importance of what is contained in the spoken text (for example, the presence and frequency of assimilation), as well as what is available to the listener, in the form of their current knowledge of second language vocabulary and syntax. It seems that lexical knowledge—in particular knowledge of how words sound in natural speech—is a greater help to second language listeners than their knowledge of grammar. How this linguistic knowledge is exploited and related to other types of listener knowledge in the processing of second language speech will be the subject of Chapter 4.

Sample recognition activities

ACTIVITY 1 Spell-guessing

This is a technique I devised to raise my students' awareness of the fact that it is easier to guess at the spelling of some words in spoken English than of others, because of the variable relationship between pronunciation and spelling in English. The materials I use for this purpose are sequences from television wildlife documentaries; I choose this particular area as none of the students in the classes I teach is likely to be a subject specialist in the topic. That means that everyone is likely to be working from a similar base.

The Spell-guessing task requires the learners to watch the section, identify all the species featured on the screen and/or soundtrack, and write down their names. Given the relatively unphonetic nature of English spelling, any spoken text is likely to contain some words that even a native speaker might have difficulty spelling. For instance, one of the wildlife programmes I have used refers to a type of sea fish called an 'eelpout' and the alpine bird 'ptarmigan'. On the other hand, there are other species mentioned in the programme, such as 'otter' and 'snow bunting', whose spelling is guessable with reasonable certainty by second language listeners.

After the Spell-guessing task, I conduct a debriefing in which I get the students to discuss the relative ease or difficulty of guessing at the correct spelling of the target items, which leads on to discussion of what tactics they can adopt in real-life lectures when they are not sure about the spelling of words used by the lecturer.

ACTIVITY 2 Trouble shooting

This technique was developed for second language learners of English by Steve Tauroza of the University of Hong Kong (Tauroza 1995). He emphasized that it was suitable as a supplementary follow-up for listening activities that required learners to listen for details—in other words, to understand specific information mentioned in one or two phrases. Trouble shooting involves three steps:

1 Identification of the problem

It is important to find out not simply how many questions learners have got right, but which of the questions they have not been able to get right.

2 Identification of the extent of the problem

The teacher needs to establish whether a point of detail represented a problem for the majority in the class, rather than just for the learners with weaker listening skills.

3 Focusing attention on the problematic parts of the message

By narrowing down to the specific sections of the listening text that have led the learners to get incorrect answers—or no answer at all—the teacher can also analyse what the precise source of the problem was. It might be any of the areas mentioned in this chapter—not identifying the (normal) spoken form of a familiar word, vowel reduction or assimilation, a new lexical item, or unfamiliar syntax.

By replaying the problematic section and by writing up the listeners' individual versions of what they have heard, the teacher can both encourage them to share their understandings and also to increase their familiarity with the troublesome point.

Suggestions for further reading

Brown, G. 1990. *Listening to Spoken English*. 2nd edition. Harlow: Longman. The classic British work on spoken language for those interested in teaching it.

System. 2008 special issue. This special issue (36/1), edited by John Field, provides an up-to-date picture of current work in listening. Five of the eight contributions relate to 'recognition' issues covered in this chapter.

Discussion and study questions

1 In the Preface I mentioned the problem I had in understanding another boy's Northern Irish accent. Do you have difficulty in understanding any particular accents of your first language? What exactly makes them hard for you to follow?

2 Are there specific sounds, or combination of sounds, in the language you teach that cause your students special problems of recognition? What can you do to make recognition easier? Is it only a question of practice, or can you help them with practical guidance?

3 Over a period of two or three weeks, make a note of any misunderstandings that you (or your students) experience. Try to analyse and identify the source of the problem. The following is an example to show you the sort of thing I mean:

My wife and I were watching a news report in 2007 about a decision by the British government to introduce electronic metal detectors, like those at airports, into some inner-city schools in London, to reduce the problem of school pupils carrying knives. A minister was interviewed and we both heard her say, 'We have decided to bring in surcharges as soon as is feasible'. Mauricéa and I then wondered who was going to pay these surcharges; it seemed unfair that schools should have to, and even more unfair that the taxpayer should. Next morning I read a newspaper report on the decision to introduce *search arches* to some London schools. (Problem: unfamiliar vocabulary, leading to incorrect lexical segmentation.)

4 INTERPRETATION

Introductory task

Below are three short utterances, which I heard in early 2008. Who do you think was speaking? Where? About what?

> I don't go up there at all + I hate seeing that restaurant up there + it's got no place being there it just disgusts me

I am now going to give you a little more context by showing you what the person had said just before the three utterances above. As you read the words, try to monitor the thoughts that go through your mind. See whether having more context to work with changes or adds to your interpretation of speaker and topic.

> there's a particular birthing tree where my great-grandmother and the women in her clan had their babies + and there are dreaming tracks around King's Park + the troopers and the soldiers came in and started shooting and uh + massacring the people and my great-grandmother and her family managed to + uh flee from there and down to the south-west + + I don't go up there at all + I hate seeing that restaurant up there + it's got no place being there it just disgusts me

What clues in the text do you use to reach your second interpretation?

Interpretations and misinterpretations

In this chapter we move from the processes by which the listener recognizes what words the speaker has used to the processes involved in interpreting the speaker's intended meaning. In doing so, our focus shifts from *what* is said to questions of 'Why that, now, and to me?', in the words of the ethnographer Harvey Sacks (Sacks 1971, quoted in Brown and Yule 1983a: 77). In Michael Rost's diagram of listening skill clusters (Table 3.1) Interpretation is the level above Perception. In everyday English we tend to use 'comprehension' and 'interpretation' to mean different things: 'comprehension' implies a straightforward process of understanding; 'interpretation' suggests a process in which the listener has to do more mental work in order to reach their own version of what the speaker meant. We talk of a text being 'open to interpretation' but not 'open to comprehension'.

The literature on listening makes clear that all but the simplest of messages involve active interpretation of the speaker's meaning. Unrevealed misinterpretations must be quite common in all our daily lives, and it is only when a listener's response shows that they have misunderstood something that a misinterpretation gets resolved—and that we may get an insight into someone else's mental processes:

> We can learn rather little about the processes of comprehension when they flow comfortably...We have an opportunity of learning rather more where understanding is difficult to come by, where interpretation is only partially achieved, or where an attempt to communicate results in misunderstanding. (Brown 1995: 42)

Cases where things do not run smoothly are useful in showing us just how far listeners have to go 'beyond the text' in order to make sense. The key question that arises is: exactly *where* does the listener go for help? The answer seems to be: to the context, to their background knowledge, and to their shared cultural values and assumptions. We will look at those in turn in the next three sections.

Context

Context provides a link between linguistic 'bottom' and non-linguistic 'top' information, as shown in Figure 4.1. When we listen to the first few sounds of a speaker's opening utterance, we may already have helpful information

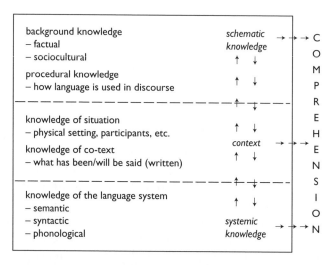

Figure 4.1 Information sources in comprehension (Anderson and Lynch 1988: 13)

about the context—about who is speaking, where they are speaking, when they were speaking (if the text is recorded), in what circumstances, and so on. We very rarely start with a completely blank contextual slate.

Once the speaker has uttered their first few sounds we also have the **co-text** to work on—in other words, what has just been said and what is still to come, together with any visual material supporting the spoken text. A couple of years ago I was watching television in Spain and heard a young woman being described as *una lanzadora de jabalina*. I knew the verb *lanzar* (to throw), the agentive ending *-adora* (marking the female doer of the action in the verb), *jabalí* (a wild boar), and the diminutive suffix *-ina*, which can be added to a feminine noun. So my first thought was that the reporter was saying that the woman was in the habit of throwing small female wild pigs around. Perhaps this was some rough country sport that I had not come across before? But then a visual clue on-screen (a photograph of a running track) indicated that this was a report about athletics, and I realized that *jabalina* must be Spanish for 'javelin', and that what the reporter was talking about was a more conventional sport than the one in my initial interpretation.

One of the first researchers to investigate the effect on second language listening comprehension of context in its widest sense, including visual support, was Dieter Wolff of Düsseldorf University (Wolff 1987), who was interested in the balance between text-based and context-based strategies used by listeners at different proficiency levels. The participants in his study were 350 German secondary school pupils aged 12–18. The listening texts were video-recordings of two stories told in English by native speakers; one was relatively easy and the other was relatively difficult. Each story came in two versions: for some listeners, a simple drawing of part of the story was inserted into the video-recording; the others watched the video without the illustration. The pupils watched each story twice and then had to recall it orally in German. When they had completed their retelling, they were interviewed about the way they had understood the text. Both recall and interview were recorded, and then analysed for three possible effects: of context (with or without the drawing), of listeners' proficiency level, and of listening text complexity.

As far as the influence of context on recall was concerned, differences emerged in listeners' use of the simple visual cues. With the easier story, the illustration had no measurable effect, but in the case of the more difficult story those listeners who had seen the drawing remembered significantly more details and also made more text-based inferences. Dieter Wolff concluded that the more linguistically demanding a text is, the greater the listener's need to exploit any available contextual cues.

In the second area of investigation—the possible relationship between processing strategies and language proficiency—the picture was less clear. The weaker listeners recalled far fewer bits of information, but when account was taken of the relative proportion of information recalled from the two stories, it emerged that the lower-level listeners had actually produced comparatively more inferences than their higher-level counterparts. In other words, they had understood less but had inferred more. On the third issue— the effect of text complexity on processing strategy—Dieter Wolff found a significant relationship between textual difficulty and story recall. The more difficult story was remembered in less detail, but with a higher proportion of inferences and invented (unrelated) information.

There appears to be considerable variation in individual listeners' use of context, as shown in two studies by John Field in Cambridge (Field 1997; 2004). In the first he video-recorded a class of seven intermediate adult learners of English as they listened to, and then discussed, an audio-recording of a story about travel documents getting lost on a holiday in France (Underwood 1976). John Field was specifically interested in the listeners' ability to deal with new or unrecognized vocabulary in the story. He found that, when asked to write down selected items, some listeners changed the words spoken to match the context: for example, the words 'mat' and 'ledge' were registered as 'map' and 'bridge', despite their apparent salience and clarity on tape.

> It is interesting that, in both cases (one of a known word, one of an unknown) clear perceptual evidence is being rejected in favour of an interpretation related to context. (Field 1997: 14)

The second study consisted of three listening experiments designed to explore the extent to which second language listeners put their trust in context-based processing, as opposed to **bottom-up** (or perception-based) **processing** of information (Field 2004). The participants were 48 EFL students in four classes at levels from higher elementary to lower intermediate. In Experiment 1 they were played groups of four to six words, chosen from among the 1,000 most frequent words in English and therefore likely to be familiar. In some cases all the words belonged to the same semantic field—for example, 'wet – cloudy – dry – cold – hot'. In others, only the final two words were linked—for example, 'big – new – empty – cold – hot'. In certain target items the beginning of the final word was changed to make it an outsider to the set: for example, 'hot' was replaced with 'got'. For Experiment 2, John Field used a contextualizing sentence in which, again, the final word was replaced with one which had one phoneme different. As before, the original and replaced words were within the 1,000-word frequency band—for example, 'The people at the party were Germans, Italians, Spanish, and some *friends*' (instead of *French*). As in Experiment 1, the listeners were asked to write down the final word in each sentence. Experiment 3 was like the second, except that the last word in each sentence was chosen to be unfamiliar to the listeners and phonologically similar to a high-frequency word. This was designed to provide a *meaningful* context for the unfamiliar word, but a *contradictory* one for the common word—for example, 'They're lazy in that office; they like to *shirk*' (instead of *work*).

The results from the first two experiments were inconclusive, but those from the third were striking. Faced with the problem of the unfamiliar word, some listeners simply left a blank space. Of those who gave an answer, just over 40 per cent rejected the phonetic/acoustic evidence of their ears—that is, that the final word was one they did not know—and matched it roughly to a word they did know. The others—a little under 60 per cent—were able to identify the item as unfamiliar and attempted to transcribe its sound shape. John Field called these two strategies 'lexical' and 'phonological', respectively, and underlined that the listeners who took the lexical route often wrote down words that were not only semantically inappropriate but also grammatically incorrect, which suggests that they were riskily adopting a strategy that is neither bottom-up nor top-down but 'potentially overrules contextual information and modifies perceptual' (Field 2004: 373).

Background knowledge

The term 'background knowledge' tends to be used interchangeably with others such as 'knowledge of the world', 'general knowledge', and 'non-linguistic knowledge'. Research has shown that the way we use this sort of knowledge in listening is essentially the same as the way we try to make sense of any perceptual input:

> Not only reading but also listening, feeling and looking are skilful activities that occur over time. All of them depend upon pre-existing structures called *schemata*, which direct perceptual activity and are modified as it occurs.
> (Neisser 1976: 14)

The word schema (plural **schemata**) originates in the work of the cognitive psychologist Charles Bartlett and has been influential in a number of fields, including research into both human comprehension and artificial intelligence (Bartlett 1932). One definition of schema in the context of listening is 'a mental structure consisting of relevant individual knowledge, memory, and experience, which allows us to incorporate what we hear into what we know' (Anderson and Lynch 1988: 139). However, as Bartlett showed in his early experiments, schemata have the power to distort, as well as support, listening comprehension and memory. Our interpretation of what we hear is often (unconsciously) modified, both at the time and in later recall, by the cognitive scaffolding that schemata provide. As soon as we examine specific instances of the way people interpret what they have heard, it becomes clear that we cannot necessarily assume that any group of listeners will share common knowledge, so the terms 'general' knowledge and 'background' knowledge raise the questions 'General to whom?' and 'Whose background?'.

When listening or reading, we construct a mental representation of the propositions (ideas) in the input; this has been called the 'textbase' (van Dijk and Kintsch 1983). At the same time we build a 'situational model' of the speaker's or writer's intended message, which is a dynamic version of the unfolding relationships between the facts, people, and objects in the text, their possible implications for us, our possible response to them, and so on. In building this mental model of the content and point of the message, we draw on information from long-term memory, using two main types of schema: **formal schemata**, which reflect knowledge of different text types or genres, and **content schemata**, consisting of knowledge of the relevant subject matter. Combining these two schema types allows the listener/reader to exploit what they know, either first-hand or second-hand, in order to interpret what they hear/read.

As a concrete example of different individuals' interpretations of the same text, let's return to the 'restaurant' text in the Introductory task. I asked 14 of my colleagues and students in Edinburgh, from a variety of first-language backgrounds, to interpret the text in two stages, as you did. As you will see in Table 4.1, their individual interpretations varied widely, and they responded in different ways to the additional contextual information in the second, longer extract.

We will come back to the issue of what is the most appropriate interpretation later in this chapter.

Research into the effects of background knowledge on second language comprehension has predominantly focused on reading, rather than listening. Overwhelmingly, the findings support schema theory: a text on a more familiar topic will be easier for readers than one on a less familiar topic (Johnson 1982); comprehension can be improved by recently gained knowledge, such as that provided by pre-reading activities, as well as by longer-established knowledge (Hudson 1982); and stories that match a formal schema are easier to read than stories that contravene the norms of narrative structure (Carrell 1984). As I noted in Chapter 2, second language

First language	Three utterances out of context	In context
1 **Japanese**	Someone who has a bad memory of the restaurant.	A Scot whose great-grandmother's folks suffered in the massacre in the glen. (I forget the name of the place.)
2 **Spanish**	Two people walking in Snowdonia in Wales.	A descendant (aboriginal? American Indian? African?) talking to someone about the massacre.
3 **German**	Someone with a deep emotional connection with the location in question. Could be a mountain in the Alps with a tourist place built on it.	More 'exotic' and further removed from my culture.
4 **English**	A hill walker, either at home in Edinburgh or standing somewhere near the Cairngorm funicular.	'Clan'—my first thoughts were Laos, Burma, areas of China. Could refer to any currently threatened indigenous group.
5 **French**	A resident of a small mountain village who has a strong attachment to his neighbourhood.	Now I'm a little confused—does 'up there' refer to a tree or a mountain? It must be a huge tree! I imagined it must be in the Alps, but obviously not.
6 **Spanish**	Someone, possibly famous... a politician, an MP, talking about the restaurant inside the National Museum or another emblematic building in Edinburgh.	Now I'm not sure the speaker is a politician...A famous historian? I think the interview took place in England but the events she talks about happened in Scotland ('up there'). The words 'south-west' and 'clan' suggest that.
7 **English**	Inhabitant of an area of natural beauty where an unsightly modern restaurant (McDonalds?) has been built on a hill with a panoramic view.	'Dreaming tracks' told me Australia and an aboriginal speaker.

(*Continued*)

Table (Continued)

8	German	A local person talking about either a prime tourist location or a point of natural beauty—the top of the Cairngorm funicular railway?	An Australian aboriginal (woman?) talking about a place of spiritual importance to her ancestors ('dreaming tracks').
9	Korean	A customer who likes the food at the restaurant but not the atmosphere and the view.	The speaker has a personal family history related to the place where her ancestors had their babies. Now she doesn't want to see it.
10	English	Member of the public—a campaigner?	She's angry because of perceived desecration of an important place—family history violated.
11	Icelandic	Someone who knows that the place where the restaurant is known for rats or mice.	I haven't changed my mind but what happened there was much more terrible than I thought. She doesn't want to have a good time where women and children were shot.
12	English	Could be anyone anywhere where the restaurant is. Does it spoil the scenery?	Now I think the speaker could be Australian aborigine, American Indian, Papua New Guinean, African. It's a symbol of intrusion of an alien and oppressive culture.
13	Spanish	A middle-aged or older person talking to a friend about a restaurant. It's quite a strong statement about the place. I can picture my mother saying something like that.	I still think it's not a young person. Probably a woman. She felt this was some sort of sacred, special place.
14	German	English. Restaurant owner who is complaining about a new restaurant which has opened somewhere near his.	Certainly not from Britain. May be he comes from India, because there some trees are seen as symbols of fertility.

Table 4.1 Comparison of interpretations of the restaurant text

listeners face additional difficulties in making sense of what they hear, compared with second language readers, especially at lower levels of proficiency. The fact that speech is typically temporary, less clearly produced and more implicit than written language means that the textbase the listener is able to create in their head will probably be less complete than one constructed by a reader, who typically has the chance to reread the printed text in front of them.

Donna Long of Ohio State University (Long 1990) compared the effects on listening comprehension of background knowledge and second language proficiency level. The listeners were 188 intermediate-level, undergraduate learners of Spanish, who were played recordings of two passages. One concerned a recent gold rush in Ecuador and served as the less familiar topic; the other was about the rock band U2. Prior to the listening experiment, Donna Long used a questionnaire to establish the individual students' knowledge of previous gold rushes and rock bands, their previous course grades in Spanish, and a self-rating of their ability to understand spoken Spanish. The students heard each passage twice, were not allowed to take notes, and were then asked to summarize in English what they had understood of the passage. This summary was a production measure of their listening comprehension. They were also given a checklist of statements on the passage topic and were asked to indicate which ones they had heard mentioned; this provided a recognition measure of their comprehension.

The questionnaire responses showed that, as expected, the learners had significantly less background knowledge about gold rushes than rock music. On the English summary recall test, they produced a significantly higher proportion of main ideas from the U2 text than from the Ecuadorean gold rush passage. However, on the checklist recognition test there were no significant differences in scores. Donna Long argued that this difference in achievement on the two measures arose because the recognition test was less challenging and because its format may have encouraged the students to guess correctly. She concluded that linguistic knowledge plays an important role when listeners do not possess the relevant background knowledge, but a lesser role when they have that knowledge available.

Of particular interest in Donna Long's paper are her 'Additional Results', reporting the recall summaries written by a small number of her undergraduate subjects (13 out of 188), which showed the distorting effects of schemata on comprehension. To use her term, these students 'over-extended' their schema of the California gold rush of 1848 and produced summaries that conflated Ecuador with California, or placed modern artefacts like plastic and Coca-Cola in the mid-nineteenth century, or merged the exploits of the Spanish conquistadores of the sixteenth century with modern-day Ecuador. Yet the students who produced these odd summaries had rated their Spanish listening ability between 'average' and 'very good'. There was similar over-extension of content schemata in some students' summaries of the U2 text, leading her to comment that 'it is clear that schemata can hurt, as well as help' (Long 1990: 73).

I found similar evidence of schema-driven distortion in a video-based comprehension experiment with 222 Portuguese elementary-level learners of English (Lynch 1988). The experiment, conducted at the British Institute in Lisbon, comprised an audio-based phoneme discrimination test, used to measure the learners' 'pure' listening ability, and a video-based comprehension test featuring a native speaker telling a story based on six pictures. At the start of the story, a small boy is on the point of going into a toy shop to buy something, when he hears a rattling tin, turns round and sees a blind man asking for money. He decides the man's need is greater than his own and puts his coins in the man's tin, just as a rich woman gets out of a car nearby and slams the door shut. The final picture shows the boy's disappointment when the blind man, assuming that the money has come from the woman, doffs his hat in her direction by way of thanks.

For the video-based test each listener had five of the pictures in jumbled order, with the last one blank. Their task was to listen to the story, number the first five pictures in order of mention, and then summarize the ending of the story in Portuguese. When I analysed the story endings written by these elementary-level listeners, I found that a sizeable proportion of them had imported information from their schemata for narratives, presumably to make up for the difficulty they had in understanding the narrative text. More than one in five (45 listeners) wrote a summary that differed from what they had heard, and produced a different ending—happy, unhappy (but for a different reason), moral, or with an unexpected twist, such as 'The boy was disappointed because the man turned out not to be blind at all' and 'The boy was disappointed when he realized that in fact the money was destined not for the beggar but for the woman standing by the car'. Such schema over-extensions showed that, faced with a relatively inaccessible second language text, some listeners had gone beyond the form of what they heard and constructed a plausible resolution, drawing on their previous experience of similar stories.

One feature of many early research studies into the possible effects of background knowledge on second language listening was that researchers used recordings of written texts read aloud, rather than natural unscripted speech. To correct that limitation, Barbara Schmidt-Rinehart of Ashland University, Ohio conducted a study intended to build on Donna Long's work by using naturally spoken prose and by testing whether background knowledge effects correlated with listeners' second language proficiency (Schmidt-Rinehart 1994). The participants in the Ashland experiment were 90 English-speaking students (in the first, second, and third quarters of a Spanish language course), who listened to two passages recorded in informal style by a native speaker of Spanish; they had to write a summary in English of what they had heard. One text concerned Hispanic universities, which was a relatively familiar topic to these students; the other was about the *paseo*, a small-town ritual in which teenagers stroll around the local park to meet members of the opposite sex—an unfamiliar topic for the Ashland students. Analysis of the first-language summaries showed a strong influence of background knowledge on the number of key facts the listeners recalled; however, this effect was not related to second language proficiency—it was equally powerful for all three groups of students.

Among the studies that have investigated how background knowledge influences second language listening, one stands out in terms of the size of its data set. In research sampling performances on roughly 150,000 listening test items in English as a second language, Amy Tsui of the University of Hong Kong and John Fullilove of the Hong Kong Examinations Authority investigated whether differences between successful and unsuccessful listening performance might result from ineffective use or over-use of either knowledge-based (top-down) or text-based (bottom-up) processing (Tsui and Fullilove 1998). They tested two possible hypotheses to explain poor listening ability. The first was that listeners' difficulties might be rooted at the 'bottom' level, in an inability to recognize words rapidly and construct an accurate representation, leading to greater reliance on contextual information and guessing. The second hypothesis was that poor second language listeners might fail because they are over-reliant on either the top-down or the bottom-up route.

Amy Tsui and John Fullilove investigated their hypotheses by analysing the examination listening scripts of 20,000 candidates in Hong Kong so as to compare scores on items where the correct response matched the likely schema, with those where the answer was in conflict with the schema. They found that the candidates who got the correct answer for 'non-matching' schema items tended to be more skilled listeners. They concluded that the less skilled listeners were able to rely on guessing in the case of matching items, but not for non-matching ones. The test data suggested that bottom-up processing was more important than **top-down processing** in discriminating the listening performance on test items.

It seems likely that background knowledge assists comprehension by freeing up the listener's mental resources, allowing more attention to be directed at processing the language input. Evidence for this comes from an experiment carried out by the psycholinguistic researcher Michael Tyler of the University of Western Sydney, who compared the responses of first and second language listeners to the same spoken texts (Tyler 2001). When they were given advance warning of the topic of the passage they were about to hear, the two groups displayed no significant difference in working memory consumption. In the absence of that prior information about the topic, the working memory consumption for the second language listeners was significantly higher than for the native listeners.

The important thing for language teachers to keep in mind is that, as noted earlier, listeners' background knowledge can distort as well as support comprehension. Knowing a great deal about a topic can lead to false interpretations if the listener does not continually monitor their current understanding against the evidence in the input—what has been called 'questioning elaboration' (Vandergrift 2003).

Sociocultural knowledge

We interpret the world through the lens of our own culture, or cultures, and listening is no exception. The culture(s) of which we are members may have very different perceptions of the same spoken text, as has been shown by a range of research studies. When a listener fails to activate an appropriate schema, leading to non-understanding, or activates an inappropriate one, leading to misunderstanding, it may be because the schema that the speaker wishes them to invoke is culturally specific and is not part of the listeners' cultural background. The speaker of the 'restaurant' text was an Australian aboriginal being interviewed on local radio; as you can see in Table 4.1, several of my Edinburgh colleagues and students recognized this after reading the longer extract. But the woman's references to 'a birthing tree' and 'dreaming tracks'—concepts which she could assume would be familiar to the radio audience—were not recognized as clues pointing to specifically Australian culture by most of the people I asked.

Most researchers looking into the effects of cultural topic knowledge on second language listening have used learners' religious knowledge and affiliations as a proxy for cultural knowledge. Paul Markham and Michael Latham investigated the cultural influence on listening comprehension of 65 adult ESL students at the University of Maryland, of whom 28 declared themselves 'religion-neutral' (knowing little or nothing about Muslim and Christian rites), 16 were practising Muslims, and the remainder were practising Christians (Markham and Latham 1987). The participants were played two recordings about prayer rituals—one in Islam and the other in Christianity. The listening comprehension scores of the Muslim and Christian subjects showed that they recalled significantly more key points from what was to them a culturally familiar text. There was also a weaker effect of familiarity on schema—namely, appropriate elaborations and over-extensions of the passage content. The students who professed no religion remembered more details from the Islamic prayer passage but also produced appropriate elaborations of the Christian one.

Chiang Chung Shing and Patricia Dunkel reported a larger-scale listening study of nearly 400 learners of English at the Chinese Naval Academy in Taiwan (Chiang and Dunkel 1992); their study focused on the potential relationship between cultural knowledge, second language listening level, and speech modifications. The students were divided by test score into two groups: low-intermediate listening proficiency (LILP) and high-intermediate listening proficiency (HILP). The test materials were two versions (Modified versus Unmodified) of two mini-lectures (Familiar versus Unfamiliar topic). The modifications made to one version of each mini-lecture involved increased content redundancy through the insertion of repetitions, elaborations, and so on. The culturally familiar topic for these Taiwanese listeners was 'Confucius and Confucianism', while the unfamiliar lecture topic was 'The Amish People'. The subjects completed a multiple-choice test featuring items mentioned in the lectures; this test not only measured their listening success, but also provided information not included in the lectures, in order to test their background knowledge. Results showed a significant interaction between speech modification and listening proficiency: HILP students benefited more from redundancy in the message that did LILP students.

In a more recent study (Markham 2001), which again used self-reported religious belief to represent cultural difference, Paul Markham explored the effect of the presence or absence of second language subtitles (captions) in videotaped materials on the comprehension of ESL learners from a variety of religious backgrounds. A total of 79 students took part in the study: 54 were religion-neutral, knowing very little if anything about Buddhism or Islam; 16 were practising Muslims; the nine others were practising Buddhists. They watched extracts from two television programmes on world religions. The first (lasting roughly nine minutes) featured Islam and the second (running for just over ten minutes) concerned Buddhism. The students watched each extract once only, with or without subtitles. The measure used to assess their listening comprehension was the number of idea units contained in their written summaries of the content of the video extracts. Summary scores showed that, in line with similar previous research, listeners' prior familiarity with the cultural content of what they watched allowed them to recall more information than from the unfamiliar material, although the results were more clear-cut for the Muslim than the Buddhist listeners. The presence of subtitles also helped the religion-neutral listeners to achieve higher scores than when they were not available.

Summary

Research into the interpretation of second language speech underlines that *what* we listen to and *why* are important influences on *how* we listen. Dieter Wolff's early study (Wolff 1987) is particularly interesting because it came at a period when teachers were being advised by classroom methodologists to encourage lower-level listeners to 'use the context'—to employ compensatory listening strategies to cope with 'difficult' speech. His findings suggested that such listeners do, in fact, guess, elaborate, and infer from background knowledge. The use, in many studies, of the learners' first language to demonstrate their comprehension of second language texts also points to the advantages of allowing language learners to use their own language when comparing their understandings. This has the advantage of enabling them to express just what they thought as they were listening; it also provides the teacher with a window on those processes en route to comprehension.

The current picture of effective second language listening that emerges from the research reported here and in the previous chapter suggests a need for balance. When language learners still have limited second listening proficiency, it is not helpful simply to encourage them to guess from context: they need to be guided to use conservative and constrained inferencing, based on context and from topical knowledge, but that also needs to be combined with principled instruction in more rapid and accurate linguistic decoding. Recognition without interpretation will be no more successful than interpretation without recognition.

Sample interpretation activities

It is easy to find examples of texts that are open to different interpretations by listeners from different cultures, or even from different generations of the same culture. Below are two that I have found work well with my students of English, in the sense of provoking lively discussion of very different individual interpretations. The procedure is very simple: I read out to the students the texts you see below, and ask them to discuss in small groups what they think the text is about, and why.

ACTIVITY 1 The System

When I first went into the System, I had to queue for ages. At first the woman did not understand what I asked for, but eventually she found the bottles I wanted. Just as I was about to pay, the red light went on. It was a good thing that I had my passport with me. (Lynch 1996a: 133)

Most listeners assume this happened at an airport. Of course, the capital S of System is not audible, so when they have heard the whole text I tell the students that it had a capital letter. In fact, it is the short name for the Swedish state alcohol shop, *Systembolaget*. When I worked in Sweden in the early 1970s, I often had to show my passport as proof of my age when I went to buy wine and beer. The red light was on the cash register and could come on either randomly or when the assistant pressed a concealed button on the floor if she thought the customer was under age. I gather the red light system is no longer in use.

ACTIVITY 2 Gravy

This one is brief and more enigmatic, and baffles (even) native speakers. My University of Edinburgh colleague Joan Cutting was the second speaker (B) in this brief conversation. Again, I ask students to say where the conversation took place and what makes them think so.

A can you tell me where the gravy is?

B I'm sorry + I'm a cyclist

If, as normally happens, they have no idea, I give them extra clues: that the two people were strangers, and that they spoke to each other in a supermarket. Solution: Speaker B was wearing a high-visibility cycling jacket, which Speaker A assumed was the uniform of a shop assistant in the supermarket.

Suggestions for further reading

Brown G., K. Malmkjaer, A. Pollitt, and **J. Williams** (eds.). 1994. *Language and Understanding*. Oxford: Oxford University Press. Particularly relevant to interpretive listening are the papers by Jean Aitchison on understanding cultural prototypes, and by Deidre Wilson on context.

Hudson, T. 2007. *Teaching Second Language Reading*. Oxford: Oxford University Press. Chapters 6 and 7 review the literature on content schemata and formal schemata, respectively, much of which applies equally to listening comprehension.

Discussion and study questions

1 Try out one of my sample Interpretation activities with a group of your students. Record the resulting discussion and analyse it for differences in interpretation. If you make a note of the interpretations, you can add them to the post-listening discussion of the next group you ask to do the sample activity.

2 If you work with colleagues from a variety of cultural backgrounds, ask them to interpret the Australian 'restaurant' text from the Introductory task—first without the fuller context and then with the additional co-text. Do any of their interpretations show similarities with those in Table 4.1? (Even if your colleagues share your first language background, they may very well offer usefully different interpretations of the text.)

3 Record a news programme in the language you teach. Replay the items and think about the amount of background knowledge each one requires the listener to bring to the text. Try to rank them in order of difficulty, according to how accessible you believe that information would be to your students. Then play the recording to a group of your students and see whether their ability to understand the items reflects the order of difficulty you predicted.

5 PARTICIPATION

Introductory task

I witnessed the incident below on a bus in Edinburgh. As you follow my description of what happened, try to decide what it was about the situation that led one listener to join in a complete stranger's telephone conversation. Why did she imitate the caller's accent? Why did the other passengers laugh?

> I was travelling on a Number 5 bus during a heavy downpour. Most of the other passengers were middle-aged or elderly women. A teenage mother got on, pushing a buggy with a small boy in it. She was wearing a light jacket, which was drenched from the rain, and her hair was dripping wet. She and her son sat down on the seat labelled 'Reserved for the elderly and infirm', three or four rows in front of where I was sitting. Two passengers behind her exchanged a glance, which I interpreted as a silent comment on the fact that the teenager had sat where she should not have done. The boy started shouting, but his mother paid him no obvious attention and concentrated on her mobile phone instead. She rang someone and when she got an answer, had to talk loudly to make herself understood above the noise from the boy. This meant that everyone on the bus could hear what she was saying. She had a strong working-class Edinburgh accent and what she said went roughly like this: 'Shona? Aye, it's me ... How're ya *daeing* (= doing)? *Ah ken* (= I know), it's terrible here, too. *Ma jaikit's* (= my jacket's) SOAKIN ... Aye. See ya later. Bye'.
>
> The woman sitting next to me looked at me, raised her eyebrows, and shook her head. I inferred she thought the phone call had been fairly pointless. Within a few seconds, the teenager was calling someone else with the same news: 'Marie? Aye, it's me ... How're ya daeing? Ah ken, it's terrible here, too. Ma jaikit's SOAKIN ... Aye ... See ya later. Bye'.
>
> This time my neighbour was frowning and tutting in annoyance. I could also see other passengers shifting in their seats and whispering to each other about (I assumed) the two loud and pointless calls. This time when she finished, the teenager put the phone back in her bag, but within about 15 seconds she had taken it out again. For the third time, she started off: 'Kelly? Aye, it's me ... How're ya daeing? Ah ken, it's terrible here, too'.

At this point the woman next to me shouted out in the direction of the teenager: 'and her jaikit's SOAKIN!'.

This brought laughter from all the passengers except the teenager, who was so intent on talking to Kelly that either she did not hear what the woman had shouted, or did not realize it referred to her.

A framework for participation

Chapters 3 and 4 focused mainly on perception and interpretation in one-way listening contexts, such as listening to the radio or watching television. In this chapter the spotlight will be on two-way listening, also known as recip-rocal, interactive, bi-directional, or conversational listening. The listener's involvement, or potential involvement, in a speaking role brings costs as well as benefits: the costs include the requirement to respond appropriately, time pressure in processing what is being said, and the risk of misinterpreting the **interlocutor**; the communicative benefits include the opportunity to get doubts cleared up and problems resolved.

The question of whether the listener is able to intervene to get help when problems arise raises the issue of whether in the particular communicative setting they feel entitled to do. In different situations the listener has differ-ent interactive rights and responsibilities: in some face-to-face situations the listener is physically able to respond but is not expected to—for instance, in the public gallery of a courtroom; in others, such as a prayer meeting, listen-ers are allowed to respond, but only in a limited and specific manner. One widely-cited analysis by the sociolinguist Allan Bell (Bell 1984) proposed four listener roles, as shown in Table 5.1.

The roles in Allan Bell's framework will vary, both between cultures and within the same culture. They are norms rather than rules, and it is possible to subvert our expected listener roles in particular cases, which is what seemed to happen in the incident on the Number 5 bus: someone who should have

Participant—someone who is being spoken to and has the same speaking rights as others present

Addressee—someone who is being spoken to but has limited rights to speak

Auditor—someone who is being spoken to but is not expected to respond

Overhearer—someone who is not being spoken to and has no right to speak

Table 5.1 A participation framework for listening (Bell 1984: 159)

been an Overhearer (the woman sitting next to me) decided to take on the role of Participant in the young mother's telephone conversation—presumably on the grounds that it had been so loud that it had involved all of us.

Bell's framework for participation was designed to apply to listening in real life, rather than in the language classroom. There, things become more complicated because the learners' role will normally be different from that of the original listener for whom a listening text was produced. For example, if a teacher uses a recording of an informal conversation in which the original listener was a Participant, our learners usually have to adopt the secondary role of Overhearers, answering questions on the content of what the interlocutors said. How listening situation and listening role intersect is shown in Table 5.2.

The role of the Participant requires a range of active listener responses. At the minimum end is 'back-channelling', the provision of feedback to the speaker on how their message is being received: acknowledgments such as 'Yeah', 'Mm-hm', and 'Uh-huh', news-marking items like 'Oh' and 'Really', and evaluative comments such as 'Wow!' and 'How terrible!'. This sort of feedback has to be thought of as part and parcel of active listening in conversation: 'There is a sense in which listener vocalisations marking receipt of previous talk, but not contributing to topic, are neither purely listening nor purely speaking' (Gardner 1998: 206). Second language learners need to be made aware of the precise intonation and use of these minimal response tokens, and how they may differ from place to place. For example, 'Uh-huh' is most frequently used by North American speakers of English, whereas

	Participant	Addressee	Auditor	Overhearer
One-way listening	—	listening to your voice mail	watching interactive digital TV	hearing someone leaving a voice mail message
Two-way listening	having a conversation	attending a lecture	listening to a live public debate	listening to other bus passengers in conversation

Table 5.2 Listening activities within the participation framework (adapted from Lynch 1996a: 93)

'Mm' is commoner in Australia and Britain. The nuances conveyed to the speaker by the intonation of the token are especially important. At the other end of the feedback scale are the more explicit and tailored expressions by which listeners signal comprehension, or the lack of it, to initiate the process by which meaning will be clarified through negotiation, as discussed in the next section.

Negotiation of meaning

There are a number of different terms used to refer to the way in which speakers adapt what they say to make themselves understandable to their audience. Among the most common are **negotiation of meaning** and **modification**. In our first language we adjust what we say and the way we say it to accommodate the listener's perspective and, to do this, we continually monitor our own speech in relation to that of our conversational partner. The modifications made for second language listeners are simply a specific case of a more general social phenomenon, with additional conversational repairs made necessary by the fact that one interlocutor is not a native speaker.

When comprehension problems occur in conversation, meaning can be negotiated in any of three ways—by modifying input, interaction, or information. The researcher most often associated with the area of native/non-native communication is Michael Long of the University of Hawaii, who used the terms **linguistic adjustment** to refer to modifications of input, and **conversational adjustment** to refer to changes in the pattern of interaction (Long 1983). In cases where both interlocutors are second language users, the negotiation of meaning may take on additional layers of complexity for them, since the current listener may not be able to rely on the other person's ability to **reformulate** or clarify something they are finding hard to understand. Extensive research into input and interaction modifications in native/non-native communication has established that interaction modifications, such as those shown in Table 5.3, have a greater effect on comprehensibility than do adjustments to input.

Building on the work of Michael Long and others into the characteristics of two-way interaction with second language users (e.g. Long 1983, 1985; Varonis and Gass 1985), three researchers from the University of Pennsylvania—Teresa Pica, Richard Young, and Catherine Doughty—investigated the effects on listening comprehension of linguistic and conversational adjustments intended to benefit the listener (Pica, Young, and Doughty 1987). They tested the hypothesis that second language listeners would achieve better understanding through interaction with a live interlocutor than by hearing a message containing **pre-modified** input. Their subjects were 16 low-intermediate learners on a general English programme,

Confirmation check
Listener makes sure they have understood what the speaker means

Comprehension check
Speaker makes sure the listener has understood

Clarification request
Listener asks the speaker to explain or rephrase

Repetition
Listener or speaker repeats their own or the other's words

Reformulation
Speaker rephrases the content of what they have said

Completion
Listener completes the speaker's utterance

Backtracking
Speaker returns to a point in the conversation, up to which they believe the listener had understood them

Table 5.3 Conversational adjustments (modifications of interaction) (adapted from Lynch 1996a: 47)

divided into an Input group and an Interaction group. The learners carried out an information-gap task in which they had to place objects on a board, following the spoken instructions of a native English speaker. The speaker and listeners sat face-to-face, with screens preventing them from seeing each other's boards. For the Input group the instructor read out a scripted set of instructions, pausing to allow the listeners time to carry out each instruction. The script was based on recordings of native speakers doing the task, with additional linguistic modifications. The Interaction group were read an unmodified script, but were encouraged to ask the native speaker for repetition, clarification, and so on when necessary. Analysis of the listeners' task performances supported the hypothesis that interaction would assist listeners more than modified input would; the Interaction listeners scored higher (through more accurate selection and placement of objects) than the Input listeners. Among the various types of interaction modification, repetition was shown to assist the listeners most.

In my Lisbon experiment, described in Chapter 4 (Lynch 1988), I investigated whether the benefits of modifications made for a second language listener in live interaction would carry over to help 'secondary listeners' watching a recording of the original conversation. The input materials were selected from video-recordings I had collected in Edinburgh of British native speakers telling picture-based stories to four different listeners in turn: first, to a native listener, and then to second language learners of English at advanced, intermediate, and elementary levels. The original listeners' task was to number six jumbled story pictures in narrative order; as they did so, they were encouraged to stop the speaker at any point to ask for clarification. For the experiment in Lisbon, I selected the stories told by four speakers whose listeners had all successfully ordered the six pictures. Without prompting from me, and without prior rehearsal, two of the speakers had adopted an input-modifying style for their original lower-level listeners, using more common vocabulary, simplified grammar, and pausing more often; and two had used an interaction-modifying style, regularly checking the listener's comprehension and responding to their doubts or queries.

Sixteen intact classes of elementary-level Portuguese learners of English each watched one of the four selected speakers telling one version of the story to one of the four original listeners. These Portuguese 'secondary' listeners were given five of the six original pictures on which the story was based, in jumbled order and with the final picture missing. Their task in the experiment was in two parts:

1 to number the pictures to match the story they watched and heard
2 to write in Portuguese what happened at the end of the story, (i.e. in the sixth picture).

The results showed that, first, their understanding of the events in the story was assisted most by watching the version told to the original listener whose level in English was closest to their own; and secondly, I found that the comprehension benefit was greater for those who watched a story told in the more interactive style, rather than one in which the teacher had tended towards a monologue of simplified input. My study showed that these secondary listeners benefited from the spontaneous modifications made for the original listener, as opposed to the controlled and scripted modifications that had been investigated in previous research.

Participation in language learner groups

We can consider language learners' 'participation' in classroom listening activities on two levels: involvement in the specific task in hand, and longer-term involvement as a member of a learning group or small culture. The American sociolinguist Claire Kramsch has written of the 'micro-world' of the second language classroom, where the language being taught is both a tool for future communication and also the instrument that shapes the social meaning of the group. In this double context

> it is through the interaction with this social group that the language is used and learnt. In turn, it is through the use of the language that the group is given a social identity and a social reality. (Kramsch 1985: 170)

This means that two-way listening tasks, in which learners are encouraged or required to interrupt each other's turns and to ask for repetition or clarification to resolve a comprehension problem, raise particular challenges of positive and negative face. A listener who has not understood what the speaker is saying has various options: to save face by waiting and seeing whether the next part of the speaker's turn will clarify the meaning, or by guessing at what they must have meant; or to risk loss of face on their own part by asking for help—for example, 'I'm sorry, I didn't catch what you said...'—or loss of face on the speaker's part by pointing to an ambiguity—for example, 'Did you say he was *shocked* or *shot*? It wasn't clear'.

Claire Kramsch makes the point that, despite the empirical evidence in favour of interactive group work from a cognitive perspective, the social dynamics of a learner group can make group work problematic, especially when a class includes individuals from different cultural backgrounds. Learners from cultures with a relatively homogeneous normative structure, such as Japan and Korea, tend to value relatively predictable behaviour. They may see less need to be verbally involved in classroom interaction with their peers, and they may feel more at home in teacher-led than learner-centred activities.

In addition to these sociocultural influences on participation, we have to bear in mind the psychological pressures on the second language learner in the classroom. Studies conducted in widely varying cultural settings have suggested that listening and speaking give rise to the greatest anxiety (e.g. Joiner 1986; Arnold 2000; Hasan 2000; Graham 2006):

> ...classes that emphasise communicative skills require active participation and a high degree of risk taking and self-exposure. Adolescent or adult learners find themselves in the uncomfortable position of trying to express mature ideas in front of their peers in an obviously still immature linguistic vehicle.
> (Arnold 2000: 777)

The balance between risk taking and non-comprehension was illustrated in a case study of an intermediate-level Japanese learner I taught on a pre-sessional English course at the University of Edinburgh (Lynch 1997). The learner, whom I called 'Kazu', had scored low on the entry listening test, compared both with his own reading and grammar scores, and also with the scores of the other students in his class. I decided to track his progress during the three weeks of his course, which included practice in two-way listening in mini-seminars. This comprised three stages—a five-minute talk by the presenter, five minutes for questions and answers, and a final five minutes for feedback. An episode from the question-and-answer stage of another student's mini-seminar will indicate how limited Kazu's ability to negotiate meaning was. When he wanted to raise an objection to a point—which he had in fact misunderstood—made by a Chinese student, 'Lian', in her presentation on the Scottish climate, it soon became clear they were talking at cross-purposes:

KAZU   I'd like to make some comment
LIAN   please
KAZU   generally the climate of Scotland is said + severe + and awful
LIAN   yes that's + the usual case
KAZU   and I think one of the reason is that the wind is very strong
LIAN   yes it usually is
KAZU   because wind is very related with our temperature + our body temperature
LIAN   hm ?
KAZU   yes + yes + so
LIAN   uh ? + you mean body temperature?
KAZU   yes
LIAN   human beings' temperature?
KAZU   yes + so + I think + the main + uh + point + uh + + + main component of + + Scottish weather is wind
LIAN   well it can never be complete when you only talk about one element + in + in climate + so I cannot say which one is the main + + figure + or main element when we talk about climate + + and I do not believe that the wind + because we are talking about atmospheric elements + conditions + so the human bodies' temperature in fact has little influence on the overall atmosphere conditions like wind + I don't think so + + + ok thank you

(Lynch 1997: 390)

What Kazu intended to say was that visitors to Scotland find the weather 'awful' because the wind reduces their body temperature, which in turn affects their meteorological perceptions. But the way he introduced the topic confused Lian, who first tried a clarification request ('hm?') and then two confirmation checks ('you mean body temperature?' and 'human beings' temperature?'), all with high-rise intonation indicating surprise. Lian's amazement was due to her having understood the *reverse* of what Kazu had meant: she thought he was saying that human body heat affects local wind strength.

In the discussions after his own presentations, Kazu appeared to adopt two basic negotiation tactics: in some cases he left the questioner to do the spadework, and in others he relied on other listeners to participate in what I called multilateral negotiation. We have an example of Kazu's leave-it-to-the-questioner tactic in the following episode from the discussion following his presentation on the current job market in Japan, when a Rwandan student, 'Paul', asked a question about Kazu's own career plans.

PAUL   under this recession + after your graduation + what kind of strategy do you have?
SS   (*laugh*)
KAZU   uh (*laughs*) pardon me?
PAUL   what kind + after graduation + + I think you are student at university?

KAZU   yes
PAUL   what kind + +
KAZU   yes?
PAUL   and after your graduation + + what kind of strategies + what kind of
          plans + will you have under this recession?
KAZU   (*laughs*) ah yes + I'm thinking about + oh + I'm also thinking about +
          taking an examination for city + officials

(Lynch 1997: 392)

Kazu's use of language is minimal; he lets Paul do most of the talking. At first Kazu laughs out of embarrassment, since clearly he has not understood why the other listeners are laughing about Paul's question—a situation that will be familiar to anyone who has failed to understand a joke in another language and has faced the 'choice between sitting tight or being the simpleton who asks for the explanation' (Harder 1980: 268).

Over the three weeks of the course Kazu made no obvious progress in his interactive listening skills and continued to rely on his peers to get his comprehension problems resolved. He did, however, make measurable improvement in one-way listening comprehension, assessed by an exit test. Three months later, at the end of the first term of his undergraduate degree course, Kazu asked for my advice over the difficulties he was having in following small-group tutorials. He said he was able to understand the tutor, but not the British students on his course. When I suggested that he should try to use the interactive listening strategies we had practised in the English course, he replied, 'But I am the only foreign student and so I cannot interrupt very much'. That comment crystallized for me a key characteristic of second language learner groups: that once a group has bonded, its members may collaborate to help each other out in negotiating meaning. On the other hand, in the world beyond the classroom—in Kazu's case, on a university degree course—second language users risk marking themselves out as less capable than the first language speakers, if they admit to not having grasped a point in discussion. In this sense, the language classroom represents a sheltered environment for the second language listener.

Participation in a second language culture

If taking part in two-way listening in the classroom can be challenging, taking on the real-life role of Participant listener in the second language culture—especially as a lone foreigner—can be even more problematic. Interesting insights into the feelings of the second language listener in this situation have been provided by two very different studies: one by a Danish speaker of English (Harder 1980) and another by an American learner of Portuguese (Schmidt and Frota 1986).

Peter Harder of the University of Copenhagen entitled his paper 'On the reduced personality of the second language learner'. It paints a very clear picture of the inevitable frustrations of trying to understand others, and to express yourself, in another language: 'the learner is not free to define his place in the ongoing interaction as he would like it; he has to accept a role which is less desirable than he could ordinarily achieve'(Harder 1980: 267–8). He described the particular social difficulties of being the only listener who does not understand a joke—and who has to decide whether or not to put the conversation on hold by asking someone to explain what was funny.

Interestingly, Peter Harder disagreed with the recommendations of the 'good language learner' literature of the time: for example, that learners should practise keeping the interaction going by saying 'Pardon me?', or by echoing expressions they have not understood, and that 'the learner should be taught not to give up in any contact he has with a native speaker' (Hatch 1978: 134). Peter Harder's view was that by exploiting conversation with a native speaker as language practice—'chaining discourse to the wheels of learning', as he put it—learners ran the risk of making themselves unpopular company:

> . . . one gets the picture of a very well-defined social role, when one imagines the learner: assiduously saying *huh* whenever there's a pause, always repeating bits of the previous utterance, blocking out interruptions by saying *uh-huh* . . . sticking like glue to unfortunate natives who said hello, etc. The picture that emerges is that of an utter pest. And this the learner, unless he's an unusually callous or charming person, is likely to be acutely aware of. (Harder 1980: 269)

In marked contrast to Peter Harder's essay, the paper on Richard Schmidt's experience as a second language learner—primarily as listener and speaker—was a detailed empirical study based on notes and recordings made over a period of five months during which he worked in Brazil and kept a journal on his progress in spoken Portuguese (Schmidt and Frota 1986). It captures the emotional ups and downs of being a second language listener in the country where the language is spoken, as illustrated in these two journal entries:

> Week 17
> Two weeks ago, M took me to a sidewalk restaurant in Copacabana to meet some friends. I've been back almost every night since . . . Between 11 and 1 about 20 regulars show up for dinner . . . They have welcomed me, and there's a critical mass of very intelligent people whom I find very stimulating. The people I've met so far have been mostly writers (journalists, novelists) or theater people (actors, producers, directors). It's a big challenge. Part of the problem is cultural . . . The language problem is severe. I frequently get so exhausted trying to keep up at least with the main topic of each conversation that I just drift off for a while. In spite of that, I've felt positively euphoric since I started to hang out there. (abridged from Schmidt and Frota 1986: 247)

Week 20
Last night I met X, who's just come back from Argentina. Before we were introduced, I overheard M and U talking to X about me at the other end of the table.
X: ele fala português? ['Does he speak Portuguese?']; *U: fala mal* ['He speaks it
poorly']. M said I make lots of mistakes . . . X saw me looking at them and said:
mas você entende tudo? ['But you understand everything?']. I was annoyed and
wanted to let them know I had been listening, so I replied: *entendo mal também*
['I also understand poorly']. (Schmidt and Frota 1986: 247)

As academic researchers in applied linguistics, Peter Harder and Richard
Schmidt were relatively high-status learners. Moreover, Richard Schmidt
was working only temporarily in a Portuguese-speaking context and knew
he would be returning to his permanent post in Hawaii. When we consider
issues of learners' participation in second language cultures, we should not
forget that many of them are likely to be low-status immigrants or migrant
workers, whose contact with native speakers may be radically different from
those of academics. An extensive investigation of immigrant listeners' participation in second language discourse was carried out in five European
countries by an international team of ethnographers—Katharina Bremer,
Celia Roberts, Marie-Therese Vasseur, Margaret Simonot, and Peter Broeder
(Bremer *et al.* 1996). Their data comprised recordings of real-life or natu-
ralistic encounters between their immigrant informants and native speakers
in a variety of gate-keeper roles, such as job interviewer and social security
officer. Investigating listening 'for real' in this way—when the Participants
are having to get to grips with spoken information in situations with a
genuine bearing on their lives—can illuminate complexities rarely revealed
in laboratory experiments or self-report surveys. The assumption underlying
the project was that

> all communication is asymmetrical given the unequal power relations in
> society . . . and that both understanding and misunderstanding are founded in
> linguistic difficulties and imbalances, social and cultural differences and
> power relations which structure individual encounters in hierarchical ways.
> (Roberts 1996: 10)

In some cases, misunderstandings are related principally to issues of language, but in most cases, the miscommunications analysed in the book are
rooted in non-shared expectations of members of different cultures, where
the expectations of the host community dominate, rather than being simply
gaps in linguistic knowledge. The way in which the second language listener's
frame of expectations influences understanding is demonstrated in the following extract, recorded in a travel agency in Marseilles, where Abdelmalek,
a Moroccan, wants to buy a ticket to Casablanca.

ABDELMALEK   *je partir a Casablanca, Maroc*
               (= I leaving for Casablanca, Morocco)

TRAVEL AGENT	*par quoi vous voulez partir?*
	(= **how** do you want to go?)
ABDELMALEK	*beaucoup problèmes là-bas papa malade + je partir tout de suite*
	(= a lot problems there dad ill + I leaving right away)
TRAVEL AGENT	*je comprends pas la + qu'est ce que vous voulez? + ou vous voulez aller?*
	(= I don't understand that + what do you want? + where do you want to go?)

(adapted from Deulofeu and Taranger 1984, cited in Roberts 1996:12–13)

Superficially, the misunderstanding turns on the travel agent's use of *par quoi* (= how), which Abdelmalek hears and understands as *pourquoi* (= why), to which he responds by explaining why he has to go back to Morocco. In a later interview with the researchers, Abdelmalek said he was used to being 'interrogated' by French people in formal encounters. So his social presuppositions as a minority member were very different from those of host community members, in that he took it for granted that the travel agent had the right to ask about the motives for his journey.

In short, this sort of qualitative ethnographic research into second language listening provides insights into the ways in which non-native listeners need to work interactively at achieving understanding, rather than being able to rely on the inferencing that is available to native listeners within the culture.

Summary

Teaching second language learners only to deal with one-way listening texts would limit their engagement with the spoken language to recognition and interpretation of what is said. Listening course designers and teachers should include activities that encourage or require them to participate in two-way listening to build up experience of the sort of negotiation of meaning that they will need to engage in to resolve comprehension problems in real-life interaction. First-hand experience of getting unclear points clarified and unfamiliar vocabulary explained helps to give learners a realistic idea of the encounters with the second language that await them in the world beyond the classroom.

Sample participation activities

ACTIVITY 1 Jigsaw speaking

This is an information-gap puzzle that can only be solved if every student in the group contributes and makes their contribution understood by everyone else. It works best with groups of six to eight listeners. You need to find, adapt, or invent a text of six to eight sentences—one for each student in the group. It needs to contain textual clues that will mark the position of the sentence in the overall sequence; below is a text I wrote for this purpose to use with elementary classes, with the clue words marked in italics.

> The QE2 is the largest passenger ship in the world. *She* can carry about **2,000** people. *They* all have beautiful cabins to sleep in. *The biggest* is about ten metres by eight. It costs four times more than *the smallest*. There are many games and sports to play during the day. There are *also* dances and discos in the evenings. It must be very nice to travel *on her*.

Write or print the sentences on a sheet of paper and cut it into separate sentence slips. Divide the class into groups of six to eight, depending on your number of sentences. You will need a set of slips for each group. Give each student one slip of paper and tell them they have **30** seconds to memorize their sentence. (Shorter or simpler sentences can be given to weaker members of the group.) Collect the slips back again and tell the students they now have to reconstruct the text without writing anything down.

The usual procedure is for each student to say their sentences aloud in turn, which should lead to interactive negotiation of meaning, since none of the learners has the complete picture to begin with. Listen in on their negotiation and make a note of the points (usually pronunciation and vocabulary) that give rise to requests for clarification or repetition.

Once they have agreed on the order, ask them to recite their sentences in sequence. If they have a correct solution, they proceed to the second stage, which is to dictate their sentences in order, so that each learner writes down the whole text.

Jigsaw speaking requires a variety of listening skills at the two stages. In the first round they are listening for overall meaning in order to establish the topic and the likely structure of the text. During the second round they listen with the advantage of having heard all the sentences, but they now have to focus on the precise form of the words in each sentence, in order to be able to convert that to written form. Typically there are questions about verb tenses, plural and singular agreement, and word order during the dictation round. The two stages of the task can only be completed satisfactorily if everyone has understood the meaning and form of every sentence, which is why Jigsaw speaking is a task that ensures participation in listening and speaking.

ACTIVITY 2 Influences on language learning (*discussion*)

It is hard to design a discussion activity that guarantees participation. One way to do it would be to set up a role play where each student is assigned a specific role and also the opinions to go with it. Far preferable to that, in my view, is to find a topic that everyone in a class is likely to have a view on; but finding such topics is not easy—in fact, Gillian Brown and George Yule went as far as to claim that the only universally interesting topics are 'power, sex and danger (real in all cases)' (Brown and Yule **1983**a: **83**). However, I find that learners' own beliefs about language learning make very successful discussion material, and the activity shown below usually provokes even the most reticent student into contributing.

Influences on language learning

Like any human activity, learning is a complex process. Which of the factors below do you think are important influences on success in language learning? Tick the ones that you feel are influential.

Knowledge of another language or other languages	
Motivation	
First language	
Gender	
Height (= how tall you are)	
Amount of language practice	
Type of language practice	
Personality	
Age	
Number of brothers and sisters	
Intelligence	

Then work with another student. Compare your ticks and choose **one** of the factors that you have ticked but the other student has not. Explain to them how you believe that factor influences success. (IALS **2008**: 1)

Suggestions for further reading

Harder, P. 1980. 'Discourse as self-expression: On the reduced personality of the second-language learner.' *Applied Linguistics* 1/3: 262–70.

Long, M. 1983. 'Linguistic and conversational adjustments to non-native speakers.' *Studies in Second Language Acquisition* 5/2: 177–93.

van Lier, L. 2000. 'From input to affordance: Social-interactive learning from an ecological perspective' in J. Lantolf (ed.). *Sociocultural Theory and Second Language Learning*. Oxford: Oxford University Press.

Discussion and study questions

1 Choose a listening textbook that you know well. (Alternatively, you can use the listening activities in a multi-skill textbook.) Using Table 5.1, decide which listener role the listening activities require learners to take on. Is it always the role of Overhearer?

2 Record a native or competent speaker of the language you teach in interaction with two of your students—one from an elementary class and the other from an intermediate class—in separate recordings. It should be the same material for the two recordings—such as a story or joke. Compare the two recordings. Does the speaker make adjustments to the listener's level? Are they adjustments of input or of interaction?

3 Record a group of students doing a Jigsaw speaking activity. What sort of problems did the listeners have as they played the first (sequencing) round and the second (dictation) round?

PART THREE

Teaching second language listening

6 LISTENING STRATEGIES AND LISTENING SKILLS

Introductory task

Here is a brief episode from a listening class in which intermediate-level learners of English as a second language were asked to guess at the meaning of unfamiliar words. The group included three students from Japan and two each from Korea and China. (The letters J, K, or C indicate which country the student was from.) As we join their interaction, the teacher is playing an audio-recording containing the word 'outstripped', chosen as a target for guessing because it was unlikely to be in the vocabulary of these listeners. As you read the episode, look for the listening tactics of the students and the teaching tactics of the teacher.

AUDIO	I suppose the third most obvious er problem for preventive medicine to tackle in the developing world / is the problem of uncontrolled population growth / there's the danger that food supplies may be outstripped by population increases
T	(*stops cassette*) so + now + + what do you think 'outstripped' means? (*waits for about five seconds*) what do you guess it means?
K I	I don't know + I never hear this before + what does it mean?
T	but that's why I'm asking you to guess! (*laughter*) + + anyone?
K I	we don't know this word + really + + please explain us
J I	you can play it again + once + once more + so we can listen well
T	no + ok what I want you to do now is + everybody write down now what you think 'outstripped' means + I'll give you five seconds to write down your guess and then ten seconds to compare what you have written (*waits for 15 seconds*) right + that's it + time's up + + what do we have?
J I	something like 'less than'
T	ok
J 2	'not enough'? maybe?
T	ok
K I	'beaten'
T	right

C1	I have 'defeated'
T2	I have 'destroyed'
T	ok
C2	'exhausted'?
J3	'less than' or 'insufficient'
T	brilliant + every one of those guesses is fine

(author's classroom data 2002)

What makes an effective listener?

When it comes to assessing someone's ability as a listener, we have to bear in mind that listening can take various forms, which make different demands on us as listeners—whether in our own language or another. Michael Rost has suggested there are four main types of listening (Rost 2002: 158): *appreciative*—for pleasure and relaxation, such as listening to music or a joke; *informational*—to gain knowledge, such as watching a travel programme; *critical*—to assess the validity or relevance of what is being said; and *empathic*—to understand someone's feelings, such as when a doctor listens to a patient or when we listen to a friend talking about family problems. Of course, those four categories are not hermetically sealed off from each other. For example, in some academic cultures university students are expected to combine informational and critical listening in lectures and seminars, and not simply to accept what they hear, but rather to be ready to question and debate.

In English, two words commonly used to describe a person's ability to listen, 'good' and 'effective', are used in different contexts and with different connotations. When we say someone is a 'good listener', what we have in mind is their competence in empathic listening; on the other hand, the term 'effective listener' is more likely to be used about informational listening. In the literature on second language listening strategies, effectiveness is related in some cases to the listener, in others to the strategy itself, or to the use of the strategy. For example, one of the first studies of second language listening strategies was entitled 'A study of the listening strategies used by skillful and unskillful college French students in aural comprehension tasks' (De Filippis 1980), showing a focus on the learners' skill in using strategies. Another, called 'A preliminary enquiry into the successful and unsuccessful listening strategies of beginning college Japanese students' (Fujita 1984), clearly assumed that it was the strategies that were effective or ineffective.

However, any strategy has to be assessed in its context of use: 'Logically, individuals will apply different strategies depending on their personality, cognitive style, *and the task at hand*' (Bacon 1992: 161, my emphasis). The effectiveness of the mental and other actions taken by a listener in pursuit of comprehension always have to be judged in relation to the specific listening activity they are engaged in, and instruction in listening strategies should be about *when* and *how* to use a particular strategy (Vandergrift 2004). For instance, using cognate words to understand spoken English may work well for a French or Italian learner of English, but less well for a Thai or Hungarian. Furthermore, it may be more effective when the French and Italian learners are listening to formal English—where Latin-based vocabulary is more common than it is in everyday conversation, which tends to feature a higher proportion of shorter words of Germanic origin. In applying listening strategies, context is everything.

Strategies for listening

Some 30 years of research into learning strategies in general, and second language listening in particular, have allowed us to build up a comprehensive taxonomy of strategies of potential value to the second language learner. In this context we should separate learning strategies (engaged in the cause of development of second language proficiency) from **communication strategies** (which are brought into service to deal with current communication problems). In the listening strategy literature, strategies are conventionally divided into three main categories: **cognitive**—used to make sense of what we hear; **metacognitive**—used to plan, monitor, and evaluate our understanding; and **socioaffective**—strategies which either involve other people in our efforts to understand, or which we use to encourage ourselves to understand. Examples of these three overall types of strategy are shown in Table 6.1.

Much of the research that has led to the construction of that taxonomy has adopted a combination of James Flavell's general learning strategy framework (Flavell 1976) and John Anderson's Information Processing (IP) cognitive model (Anderson 1985), mentioned in Chapter 1, with its three stages of Perception, Parsing, and Utilization. The dominant influence of Anderson's model has had two main effects on listening strategy research. Firstly, it has dictated the terms in which researchers have analysed their data. For example, in one much-cited piece of research, Michael O'Malley, Anna Uhl Chamot, and Lise Küpper used the IP approach to investigate the strategies used by eight Spanish-speaking learners in high school ESL classes in the north-east United States (O'Malley, Chamot, and Küpper 1989). The students had been nominated by their teachers as either effective or ineffective listeners on the basis of various criteria: attentiveness in class; ability to follow directions without asking for clarification; the ability to understand the gist of a difficult listening text; the ability to respond appropriately in conversation; and the ability and willingness to guess at the meaning of unfamiliar words. The researchers found that during Perception the effective listeners in the group were more aware of problems of attention and attempted to deal with them; in the Parsing stage the effective listeners used more top-down,

Cognitive	Metacognitive	Socioaffective
Predicting/inferencing • from the text • from the voice • from the body language • between discourse parts	**Planning** • advance organization • self-management	**Questioning** (two-way tasks) • asking for clarification • asking for repetition • using comprehension check
Elaboration • from personal experience • from world knowledge • from academic learning • from imagination	**Comprehension monitoring** • confirming comprehension • identifying words not understood	**Cooperation** • working with other learners
Contextualization	**Directed attention** • concentrating • persevering despite problems	**Anxiety reduction** • encouraging yourself • comparing yourself with others • focusing on success
Imagery	**Selective attention** • listening for familiar words • listening for the overall message • noticing the information structure • noticing repetition and reformulation • listening to specific parts	**Relaxation** • using physical techniques • using visualization
Summarization • mental • physical (notes)		
Translation		
Repetition		
Transfer from other language(s)		
Deduction	**Evaluation** • checking interpretation against predictions • checking interpretation against knowledge • checking interpretation against context	
Fixation • stopping to think about spelling • stopping to think about meaning • stopping to memorize		

Table 6.1 Listening strategies (based on Goh 2002; Vandergrift 2003; and Kondo and Yang 2004)

knowledge-based strategies than bottom-up, input-based strategies; and that in Utilization the effective listeners related the input they heard to their own experience and background knowledge. The researchers reported significant differences between the effective and ineffective listeners in their self-monitoring, elaboration, and inferencing.

The second effect of the dominance of the IP model has been to emphasize the cognitive and metacognitive strategy types and to underplay the

socioaffective strategies. In fact, the term socioaffective is something of a ragbag, since it conflates social strategies, which may be available and appropriate in a two-way interactional setting, (for example, asking for repetition, asking the speaker to slow down), and the affective strategies that are internal and private (such as encouraging yourself to believe you can cope with a particular text, or telling yourself that other listeners have greater problems than you do). Although a small number of studies have focused on strategy use in interactive contexts, where social listening strategies are possible (e.g. Rost and Ross 1991; Lynch 1995; Bejarano, Levine, Olshtain, and Steiner 1997; Lam and Wong 2000), they are much less common than strategy research in one-way listening contexts. However, it seems likely that the current growing interest in Sociocultural Theory (SCT) will bring an expansion of interactive listening strategy research from an SCT perspective.

Arguments over strategies

Understanding the literature on listening strategy research is not straightforward, because of the debates over terminology and over the benefits claimed for listening strategy instruction. Of those controversial issues, I will briefly mention two: the relative status of strategies and skills, and the question as to whether strategies are teachable at all.

Strategies or skills?

This particular debate was encapsulated in the exchange of views between Tony Ridgway and John Field (Ridgway 2000; Field 2000), which was partly related to the wider issue of whether strategies are conscious or unconscious. In their pioneering collection of papers on second language communication strategies, Claus Faerch and Gabriele Kasper had described strategies as 'potentially conscious plans' (Faerch and Kasper 1983: 36) and a later review of the concept of strategy had concluded that strategy use involves 'some degree of conscious awareness on the part of the learner' (Oxford and Cohen 1992: 9). However, Tony Ridgway argued that there can be no clear distinction between what is conscious and what is not (Ridgway 2000). Moreover, what is a conscious action for one person may be unconscious and automatic for another. He went on to say that strategy instruction may result in teachers undervaluing or disregarding the role of practice, and he cited a study of reading strategies (Robb and Susser 1989), which had found that a group of second language learners that received training in reading strategically had, in fact, made *less* progress than a group that had engaged in reading practice but without strategy instruction. Tony Ridgway concluded that teaching cognitive strategies such as guessing is a waste of lesson time, since in real-life (one-way) listening, second language learners do not have enough spare processing space to use strategies in real-time listening. He did, however, accept that it made sense to teach the use of negotiating strategies for clarifying in two-way conversational listening.

In his response to Tony Ridgway, John Field argued that it was essential to distinguish between the terms 'skill' and 'strategy' (Field 2000). He defined a skill as an ability that the first language listener possesses and uses automatically, but which a second language listener has yet to acquire; and a strategy as a technique that the second language listener resorts to, consciously, to compensate for incomplete second language knowledge or ability, and which has caused a problem of comprehension. In an earlier paper (Field 1998), he had proposed a remedial approach to teaching listening—similar to Steve Tauroza's trouble shooting technique (see Chapter 3)—in which the teacher uses learners' performance on a listening task to establish precisely which sub-skills have caused problems of perception or interpretation, in order to devise micro-exercises to practise the relevant sub-skills.

Can listening strategies be taught?

Researchers have now found some evidence of a relationship between second language listeners' strategic awareness, strategy use, and listening performance. However, there is much less evidence for the positive effects of strategy *training*, in terms of improved listening. Among the researchers who have investigated the role of cognitive and metacognitive listening strategies are Larry Vandergrift and Christine Goh (Goh 1997, 2000, 2002; Vandergrift 1999, 2003; Goh and Taib 2006; Vandergrift, Goh, Mareschal, and Tafaghodtari 2006), using a variety of methods including learner diaries, learner interviews and questionnaires, and retrospective recall. Given the invisible nature of the listening process, researchers have to rely on learners' self-reports, as they have no way of achieving an objective view of what is going on inside listeners' heads. The disadvantage is that investigations based on self-reported behaviour are inevitably one step removed from the behaviour itself.

From the point of view of the language teacher, the study by Vandergrift, Goh, Mareschal, and Tafaghodtari (2006) appears to represent the most tangible outcome from two decades of research into metacognitive strategy use in listening. Drawing on the findings of a wide range of previous work, the researchers developed, tested, and validated their Metacognitive Awareness Listening Questionnaire (MALQ), which underwent extensive trialling by almost 1,000 second language learners in Canada, Singapore, and the Netherlands. When these listeners' self-report responses were correlated with their performances on listening tests, statistical analysis showed that five factors derived from the MALQ responses appeared to correlate with listening ability: Problem-solving (guessing and monitoring those guesses); Planning and Elaboration (preparing for listening and assessing success); Mental Translation—or, rather, avoiding it; Person Knowledge (confidence or anxiety, self-perception as a listener); and Directed Attention (ways of concentrating on aspects of the task). Taken together, these five factors were found to account for some 13 per cent of the variability in the listeners' performance, which the researchers described as a moderate relationship. (However, another way of looking at the outcome is that almost 90 per cent of success in listening appeared to be down to other factors.)

Larry Vandergrift and his colleagues suggested that the statistical relationship between those five principal factors is evidence for the complex and interrelated nature of metacognitive processes in listening, and they used the term **orchestration** to refer to the process by which the learner has to coordinate different aspects of strategy use. In choosing that word, they were echoing some of the earliest work on learning strategies, where metacognition was described as 'active monitoring and consequent regulation and orchestration of these processes in relation to the cognitive objects or data on which they bear' (Flavell 1976: 232).

Among the handful of studies of socioaffective listening strategy instruction, the most widely cited is a study of Japanese learners of English by Michael Rost and Steven Ross (Rost and Ross 1991). Its starting point was the belief, discussed in Chapter 5, that the key to second language development is the opportunity for conversation in which the learner communicates with a native (or more proficient) speaker of the language:

> learners need not only to be in an optimal input-rich environment, but they may also need the right people—and probably also the right topics—to test out their developing understanding and production abilities in the target language. (Rost and Ross 1991: 236)

From previous research, there was evidence that second language learners progressed through three stages of interactive listening strategy use. At the elementary stage, listeners use **global** queries such as 'Uh?' and 'I don't understand' to indicate problems of comprehension, without a clear indication of the source of difficulty. At the intermediate stage, they use **local** listener queries to focus on a current problem of understanding. The third stage of development is marked by clarification questions using an **inference**, marking a shift from understanding at local level towards understanding at discourse. The extract below features three international students attending an English speaking class in Edinburgh—Isabel from Spain, Yuko from Japan, and Khalid from Malaysia. Khalid's contributions, shown in bold, illustrate all three of the interactive listening strategies underlying the Ross and Rost research. As we join them, Isabel is talking about Seville, her home city.

ISABEL	I was telling one of my friends + 'yeah we have all the streets full of orange trees' and + he asked me + 'but don't you eat the oranges?' + 'no they're very bitter it's impossible they're + really bitter' and + do you know
YUKO	it must be wild one + + wild orange tree + + + wild
KHALID	**huh?** *[global strategy]*
ISABEL	wild?
YUKO	yes so nobody tries to eat them + the oranges from + uh +
ISABEL	the street?
YUKO	the street yes
ISABEL	no no + but do you know why do you use that orange for?
YUKO	for marmalade
KHALID	**what?** *[global strategy]*
YUKO	marmalade + sweet sort of jam
ISABEL	yeah but for the + + queens of England but not for us + we don't use it at home + + just to threw to each other
KHALID	**threw?** *[local strategy]*
YUKO	(*laughs*)
ISABEL	yeah it's true + at Christmas I was having a party with my friend + + just a dinner very quiet + and suddenly + + we went in the + balcony
KHALID	hmhm
ISABEL	somebody throw at us an orange
YUKO	ah!
ISABEL	it went (*makes sound effect*) POOSH! to the wall
KHALID	**is that traditional way to + + celebrate something or what?** *[inferential strategy]*
ISABEL	no
KHALID	**just to + + annoy** *[inferential strategy]*
ISABEL	to bother us (*laughter*)

(*author's classroom data 1997*)

The participants in the Rost and Ross investigation of these three stages were 340 Japanese college students, divided into equal numbers of lower- and higher-proficiency listeners on the basis of a test. Phase 1 of the study involved eliciting listener queries from the students as they heard a story told to them one-to-one by a native speaker. These queries were found to confirm the three-stage pattern described in previous research above and to be related to individual listening proficiency level. Phase 2 was an experiment for which the students were divided into four cohorts. Two modes of story presentation were employed—either distant (viewing a videotaped story) or live (one-to-one)—and three types of prior training in questioning strategies (global, local, and inferential). The results showed that proficiency level was significantly related to the success of the strategy training. The higher-proficiency listeners were able to formulate inferential questions relatively easily, presumably because they had more processing capacity spare to allocate attention to the overall development of the story. The lower-proficiency listeners, 'lacking a critical mass of lexical knowledge' (Rost and Ross 1991: 262), needed to devote more processing capacity to specific word meanings, and found it difficult to formulate inferential questions. Overall, the study showed that the natural use of certain interactive listening strategies correlates with second language proficiency, but that questioning strategies can be successfully taught to learners who might not otherwise use them.

Although we do have some evidence that strategy instruction can be successful, there remains an element of doubt, with opinions divided between enthusiastic—and mainly North American—advocates of strategy instruction, and more sceptical voices that point to the lack of clear evidence that such instruction actually produces more effective listeners, as opposed to more self-aware listeners or more knowledgeable listeners. One leading proponent of a strategic listening approach, David Mendelsohn, argues that the disappointing findings of listening strategy research until the mid-1990s arose because the strategy training programmes under study lacked one or more of five essential features of successful intervention: in-depth teacher education in the efficacy of strategy use; a strong teacher commitment to a strategic approach; the gradual implementation of strategic instruction, maintained over time; a consistent focus on the listening process, i.e. on how to listen; and the use of video rather than audio materials (Mendelsohn 1998: 84).

Among the more sceptical commentators on the effectiveness of training in communication and learning strategies in general are Jane Rees-Miller (Rees-Miller 1993) and Ian Tudor (Tudor 1996). Jane Rees-Miller argued that a learner's actual use of strategies is much more complex than most researchers had recognized, being open to a wide range of psychological, educational, sociocultural, and contextual influences, so that it would be over-simplistic to attempt to get learners to imitate the behaviour of individuals identified as 'good language learners'. Similarly, Ian Tudor warned that 'it would be misleading to assume that strategies can be neatly pedagogised and "taught" to learners in a straightforward manner' (Tudor 1996: 39).

As far as strategic instruction in listening is concerned, John Field noted three reasons for caution in interpreting the apparently positive results of listening strategy research (Field 1998). The first was that, at the time he was writing, only a small minority of the explicit training studies had produced clear findings. Secondly, the classification system used by most strategy researchers (Oxford 1990) was oriented more towards longer-term learning and did not distinguish between strategies used for learning and those used for short-term comprehension. Thirdly, willingness to use strategies might reflect individual personality and cognitive style: 'a view could be taken that the aim of strategy training should not be to teach a uniform set of procedures but to encourage the reluctant strategy-user and restrain the rash' (Field 1998: 116).

It could well be that second language listeners' use of strategies is to some extent determined by their home culture. There is wide agreement that culture exerts a key influence on individuals' learning processes in general and on their language learning style and learning strategies (e.g. Oxford and Anderson 1995; Oxford 1996). Research into cultural learning styles has tended to follow sociological and sociopsychological work on a broader canvas, such as that of Geert Hofstede (Hofstede 1980). One of the dimensions used to position one culture in relation to others is 'tolerance of ambiguity' (TOA)—the willingness of members of a culture to accept uncertainty, vagueness, and fuzziness. According to Oxford (2002), cultures with a low TOA resort to rules and regulation to avoid uncertainty, while high-TOA cultures are open to change and taking risks. Since guessing is a form of communicative risk-taking, it would be interesting to research the possible implications of TOA for second language learners' willingness to guess at meaning when they encounter unfamiliar or ambiguous input. Learners from low-TOA cultures in East Asia are often said to be noticeably more reluctant than others to guess at the meanings of unfamiliar words—or, rather, are reluctant to share their guesses in front of the class, which may be a rather different thing. Colleagues of mine who have taught English in Japan, for example, have told me that the local cultural orientation to the group, rather than the individual, can have the effect that Japanese learners hesitate to venture an answer that they think might be incorrect, and prefer to stay silent, waiting to see what answer emerges by consensus.

One thing that writers of all shades of opinion agree on is the pressing need for long-term research to assess how listening strategies develop over time, with or without explicit training. Among the likely reasons for the lack of longitudinal research are the methodological difficulty of isolating the possible effects of such instruction from other real-life influences, and the fact that learners naturally improve their second language proficiency over time, which may help make them better listeners, irrespective of any strategic training. Suzanne Graham, Denise Santos, and Robert Vanderplank monitored the progress over six months in listening strategy use by two English secondary school learners of French, chosen because of their high and low scores on a listening test (Graham, Santos, and Vanderplank 2008). Their strategy use was investigated by asking them to give a 'running commentary' of their thoughts in the process of doing a multiple-choice listening test. Analysis of their commentaries showed that there was very little change in their strategy use over the six months, leading the researchers to conclude that listening strategy use is relatively stable and closely tied to proficiency level.

Summary

There is general agreement that the key to successful strategy training is to find ways of involving the learners in the instruction process and to draw on their (different) individual experiences of second language listening tasks:

> We must be very careful not to make the assumption that our students do not use strategies. After all, everyone has strategies that they use; what we must find out is what these strategies are. (Mendelsohn 1995: 135)

The checklist below brings together the recommendations of classroom-oriented listening strategy research from the last two decades:

- Find out what strategies your students already use. Do not assume that you know.
- Make sure your students are aware that not all listening tasks require the same strategies and that they will need to be flexible in their approach to any given task.
- Focus on a small number of strategies—ones that you have found your students are underusing or not using at all.
- Use yourself as a model for using a strategy. Talk the class through your own internal strategic processes as you listen to a difficult text. After giving the students a practical illustration of this sort of think-aloud technique, get them to do the same in pairs with a listening text.
- Follow up classroom listening activities with a 'debriefing' discussion of the strategies the learners have used. Make this cycle of practice–comparison–evaluation–practice a regular part of your listening instruction.
- Encourage students to practise these listening strategies for themselves outside the language classroom. For example, ask them to keep a listening diary, reflecting their experiences with different types of listening task.
- Include practice in interactive listening strategies in conversation activities. Choose tasks likely to lead to natural negotiation of meaning and therefore the use of 'listener queries'.

(Based on O'Malley, Chamot, and Küpper 1989; Bacon 1992; Chamot 1995; Lynch 1995; Laviosa 2000; Vandergrift 2004)

Sample strategic listening activities

ACTIVITY 1   Listening to an unfamiliar language

It can be difficult at first to get some students to talk about their listening strategies; they may simply blame themselves for being poor listeners. But using a listening text in a language they do not know is one way of 'forcing' them to use compensatory strategies. Some years ago I compiled a series of British television soundtrack extracts from foreign language interviews broadcast with English subtitles, featuring speakers of Finnish, Bengali, and Kogi (an indigenous Colombian language). I chose the extracts because the background sounds offered potential clues to help listeners make sense of what was being said. The Finnish speaker was a factory worker talking about manufacturing practices; the Bengali extract involved a farmer talking, in increasing distress, about the recent loss of her land; and the Kogi speaker was a girl of eight or nine talking to the chickens she was looking after and then scolding one of them as it tried to get into her family's house.

The questions I set for this sort of activity are:

> 'What mental picture do you get of the speaker?'
> 'In what sort of location do you think they were recorded?'
> 'What are they talking about?'
> 'What emotions were they feeling at the time?'

After discussing these three examples, I played the students a recording of a man talking in an unfamiliar dialect (the Doric of rural Aberdeenshire). I did not tell them it was English; my aim was that they should realize they could recognize just enough of his words to know that he was talking 'aboot life on a hell ferem' (= *about life on a hill farm*).

Asking the learners to compare their responses to listening texts in which the language sounds are totally unfamiliar provides a good platform for them to talk about the clues they have picked up as they tried to construct a mental model of what they were hearing.

ACTIVITY 2   Using a strategy checklist

In *Study Listening* (Lynch 2004), drawing on the work of Michael Rost (Rost 2002) and Larry Vandergrift (Vandergrift 1999), I designed listening practice in six 'macrostrategies': Predicting, Monitoring, Responding, Clarifying, Inferencing, and Evaluating. Each strategy is introduced, practised, and discussed in separate units and then, in the final units of the course, the learners use a strategy checklist (Table 6.2) to support their listening to a lecture on climate change.

Predicting
Do you expect the lecturer:
• to say that climate change is not serious?
• to tell us about alternative methods for measuring climate change?
• to say that recent policies have been successful?
• to argue that the environment can recover?

Monitoring
Monitor your understanding of what is said and the ways in which the lecturer helps that process:
• by outlining the structure of the talk.
• by marking the sections.
• by directing our attention to the key points.
• by emphasizing the contrasts between alternatives.

Monitor parts of the talk where you are less certain—then see Clarifying.

Responding
As you take notes, think about your personal response to what has been said.
• Do I accept that these 'facts' are true?
• Do I think these views are reasonable?
• Do these claims match what I know?

Clarifying
As you monitor the points that are not clear, prepare questions that you would like to ask the lecturer:
• I didn't catch what you said about . . . (X).
• I didn't understand what you said about . . . (X).
• I don't quite see how (X) relates to (Y).

Guessing
Don't expect to understand everything. Make reasonable guesses by exploiting:
• your general background knowledge.
• your knowledge of the lecture topic.
• the context and co-text (what has just been said).
• your knowledge of English vocabulary and grammar.

Evaluating
Take time to assess your listening performance:
• Have I understood the main points?
• Have I been able to follow the argument and the examples?

Table 6.2 Checklist for integrating the macrostrategies (Lynch 2004: 208)

The checklist is designed to help listeners to orchestrate their listening strategies, first as they prepare for the listening, then as they make notes on the lectures, and finally—in the follow up to the listening—as they ask clarifying questions (for discussion by other students and the teacher), critique the lecture content, and evaluate their own listening performance. In terms of the research reviewed and discussed in this chapter, the students are guided through the application of the three broad types of listening strategy: cognitive (Predicting, Inferencing, and Responding), metacognitive (Monitoring and Evaluating), and socioaffective (Clarifying). The checklist can be adapted to any sort of talk requiring informational listening.

Suggestions for further reading

McDonough, S. 2006. 'Learner strategies: An interview with Steve McDonough.' *ELT Journal* 60/1: 63–70. A realistic and very readable account of the difficulties, findings, and implications of strategy research for second language teaching.

Mendelsohn, D. 1994. *Learning to Listen: A Strategy-based Approach for the Second-language Learner.* San Diego, CA: Dominie Press. A book for teachers which sets out a coherent and comprehensive programme of listening strategy instruction.

Vandergrift, L. 2003. 'Orchestrating strategy use: Toward a model of the skilled second language listener.' *Language Learning* 53/3: 463–96. A case study of a small group of learners of French. The qualitative analysis of their individual patterns of listening strategy use makes the paper especially relevant to the practising teacher.

Discussion and study questions

1 Select or design an interactive communication task suitable for pair work (for example, the Describe and draw map task shown in Chapter 9). Record a pair of your students doing the task and then listen for instances of the three listening strategies featured in the Rost and Ross study—global, local, and inferential. If possible, make a second recording with a pair of students at a different proficiency level or in a different school year. Can you find evidence of development over those three stages?

2 Read again the recommendations in the Summary section. Discuss with your teaching colleagues whether it would be feasible to introduce listening strategy training for your students. If you had time for, say, just six short training sessions, which six strategies from Table 6.1 would you include?

3 'The individual nature of strategy use ... suggests a role for a mode of instruction that begins with an analysis of current strategy use (in terms of how strategies are used, rather than which ones or how often) and which includes individual feedback from the teacher on how well strategies are being employed' (Graham, Santos, and Vanderplank 2008: 67). What techniques would you use to identify your second language students' listening strategies?

7 LISTENING MATERIALS AND LISTENING TASKS

Introductory task

Is the text below the transcript of an actual radio weather forecast, or is it an invented text? What clues influence your decision?

> hello Charlotte yes well it's + looking pretty reasonable for the bank holiday weekend for a change + + if we take southern England the Midlands and East Anglia first + mainly clear skies with sun for the better part of the day clouding over towards the evening but it should stay mainly dry + + for Wales northern England and Northern Ireland milky cloud first thing and then some light drizzle in the late morning + but then heavier showers marching in in the afternoon and more organized rain setting in by the evening + + Scotland should have the best of the weather today bright sunshine + for most of the day with clear skies in most parts + just a chance of some light showers flirting with the north-west coast and Northern Isles + temperatures again not bad for May low teens in England Wales and Northern Ireland and high teens in Scotland with a good chance of 21 or 22 degrees around the Moray Firth + and that's your holiday weather + looking over the next week or so mainly high pressure so it's going to be clear skies or high cloud for most of us + but still a chance of some quite chilly nights and a touch of frost in some of the Highland glens so we're not quite out of the woods yet + and now back to you Charlotte

Critiquing listening materials

The year 1983 marked a watershed in second language listening materials development, with four academic publications that changed the way in which we now approach listening instruction. Two were books by Gillian Brown and George Yule, who were then based in Edinburgh: *Teaching the Spoken Language* (Brown and Yule 1983a) and *Discourse Analysis* (Brown and Yule 1983b); the other two were journal articles by Michael Long, on the conversational adjustments made to non-native listeners (Long 1983), and by his University of Hawaii colleague Jack Richards, on approach, design,

---

Content validity
Does the task practise listening (or something else)?
How closely does the input or tasks relate to the relevant micro-skills of listening?

Comprehension or memory
Does the task focus on the processing activities of comprehension or on the
retrieval of information from memory?

Purposefulness and transferability
Does the task approximate to real-life listening purposes?
Do the skills practised transfer to real-life listening?

Testing or teaching
Does the task provide practice for *existing* listening skills?
Does it help the learners to acquire *new* skills?

Table 7.1   Criteria for evaluating listening tasks
(adapted from Richards 1983: 233–4)

and procedure in teaching listening comprehension (Richards 1983). I have
already referred to the first three in earlier chapters, so here I will concentrate on the way in which Jack Richards' work has influenced the design
of listening materials. His 1983 article reappraised the principles of second
language listening instruction, drawing on research in psycholinguistics,
cognitive science and discourse analysis, and in particular on work on the
role of schemata. His analysis of listening into micro-skills provided the basis
for Michael Rost's framework of listening skill clusters, discussed in Chapter
3 (Table 3.1), and the article also offered helpful criteria for critiquing listening tasks, shown in Table 7.1.

The quarter of a century since Jack Richards' 1983 article have seen significant developments in various areas of second language acquisition research,
such as the negotiation of meaning. In two recent articles (Richards 2006,
2007) he has taken account of research into input-for-comprehension and
input-for-learning in his proposal that listening instruction needs to be
extended into cycles of two phases—the first concentrating on the extrac-
tion of meaning (comprehension) and the second to include noticing and
restructuring activities (learning). Interestingly, this can be seen as a return
to an older tradition of second language listening instruction in which listening activities were followed by language study: the book *Varieties of Spoken
English* (Dickinson and Mackin 1969), for example, used audio material in
just this sort of two-phase structure, and more recently Leni Dam Jensen proposed a similar approach to video-based comprehension (Dam Jensen 1996).
My own work in listening materials design has taken the same direction;
the second edition of *Study Listening* (Lynch 2004) includes post-listening
noticing tasks, using transcripts of the listening input. We will come back to
'focus on form' as a post-listening activity later in this chapter, in my Design
example.

Adapting and improving listening tasks

As with any teaching material, if a teacher decides that a particular set of listening material is deficient in some respect, it may be possible to adapt or supplement it. In his comprehensive analysis of the intricacies of materials evaluation and design, my former colleague Ian McGrath, now at the University of Nottingham, defined three types of adaptation—extemporization, extension, and exploitation (McGrath 2002). 'Extemporization' is a teacher's spontaneous response to a problem, such as deciding to replace an unfamiliar linguistic item in an exercise with one that is closer to the learners' culture; these extemporizations tend to be immediate and oral. 'Extension' involves giving students further examples to enhance their understanding— 'more of the same'. 'Exploitation' is the teacher's creative use of published material to serve a different purpose than the materials writer intended.

In Ian McGrath's terms, Jack Richards' 1983 article offered an 'exploitation' of existing published listening material. He reported how a group of trainee teachers attending one of his workshops in Hawaii had adapted materials from *Have you Heard?* (Underwood 1979). After some workshop input on schema theory and other recent developments, the trainees were given Mary Underwood's material and asked to suggest changes in the way they would use it with their own students of English as a second language. Before we see their alternative proposal, here is a transcript of the listening passage they were discussing:

> FELIX So there was no *great l, lengthy process* of deciding what I was going to do. But I don't feel I've made a mistake. I enjoy it. I enjoy the company of other members of the *staff* in the staff room where … they … are colleagues of yours b, but you're not in *a structured system* where they are your *boss* or you are theirs. Everyone is *in the same boat*. Everyone is in the same level, and yet you don't actually work with one another. You just work with the same boys and therefore, I think, that unlike an office situation you … get to know them, other members of staff as friends more as *workmates*. And also I enjoy the, the difference of the job. It isn't the same thing every day. It's th, the same thing every year but i, in, in a yearly situation you can do things a different way in a, in the second year and the third year you do it. And I enjoy the, the difference that it brings, every day, different classes, different *age groups*, different attitudes.

(Underwood 1979: 177, my italics)

This was the first of three interview extracts in a unit on people talking about their jobs. In the original textbook, the learners prepared for listening to Felix talking about being a school teacher by reading, first, a short synopsis of what they would hear and then explanations of seven words and expressions (italicized in the transcript above). On first listening, they heard the extract and answered eight true/false questions. During their second listening, they had to identify synonyms for six other expressions. The third task was to transcribe a short excerpt. The adapted version produced by Jack Richards' trainees featured the following activities:

Pre-listening (to activate schemata and vocabulary)
– Learners discuss what makes a job enjoyable.
– They rank their findings.
– They discuss the pros and cons of school teaching.

First listening (for gist)
Learners have to find answers to the questions 'What is Felix's job?' and 'Does he like it or not?'.

Second listening (more detailed)
'Which of the following topics does Felix say are important?' (list of six topics)

Third listening
Learners answer five true/false questions.

Post-listening (inferring from context)
For example, 'What is the meaning of the expression "to be in the same boat"'?
(*adapted from Richards 1983: 237*)

In the light of Jack Richards' recent call for listening course designers to provide a dual focus on listening-for-comprehension and listening-for-learning (Richards 2007), it is interesting to speculate on what changes a group of his trainees today might make to the same materials, in the form of second-stage or post-listening activities. For example, one possible focus-on-form listening exercise would be to ask the learners to identify the various links in the chain of referring to 'people one works with' ('members of staff', 'colleagues', 'boss', 'workmates'), which was, in fact, in Mary Underwood's original textbook. Another would be to discuss what Felix really meant by 'the difference of the job', since it might have been more accurate to have said 'the variation in the job'.

Widening the scope of listening tasks

One of the most noticeable changes in the design of second language listening materials over the last 30 years has been the gradual expansion of the range of questions and tasks. Listening courses in the mid-1970s tended to focus on literal comprehension tasks that required the learners to identify information explicitly stated by the speaker, in other words to work at the recognition level of comprehension discussed in Chapter 3. For example, the popular British listening book *Viewpoints* (O'Neill and Scott 1974) contained an interview with an automation specialist discussing the effects of repetitive assembly line work on factory workers. The questions the learners were asked at the end of one section of the interview were these:

1 On this particular assembly line, what do the girls do?
2 What does the first girl do?
3 Mr Thurlow mentions another girl. What does she do?
4 What 'mechanism' is Mr Thurlow talking about?
5 How difficult is the operation?
6 How many times a day would a girl do the same thing on the machine?

(*O'Neill and Scott 1974: 85*)

All the information needed to give correct answers to those six questions was available in the spoken input, so the listeners did not need to go beyond the text—to infer or to interpret—in the ways we considered in Chapter 4.

Developments in research into comprehension—both reading and listening—in the early 1980s worked their way through to classroom methodology texts such as Christine Nuttall's book on teaching second language reading skills (Nuttall 1982), which extended the scope of comprehension questions to include interpretive and reactive tasks, resulting in six types of question:

Literal comprehension
where the answer is stated explicitly in the input

Reorganization
where the answer can be assembled from information in different parts of the input

Inference
where the answer is implied in the input

Evaluation
where the listener is asked to assess whether the speaker's communicative aim was achieved

Response
where the listener is asked to give a personal reaction to what was said

Metalinguistic question
intended to raise learners' awareness of language forms used by the speaker

---

Table 7.2 Comprehension question types (adapted from Nuttall 1996: 188–9)

The horizons of listening comprehension have recently been extended still further by developments in areas such as listening strategy use, socio-cultural theory, and critical language analysis. Taking these into account, John Flowerdew and Lindsay Miller of the City University of Hong Kong have offered an updated model of second language listening comprehension (Figure 7.1), which teachers can use as a checklist for evaluating and critiquing existing materials or for designing their own listening materials.

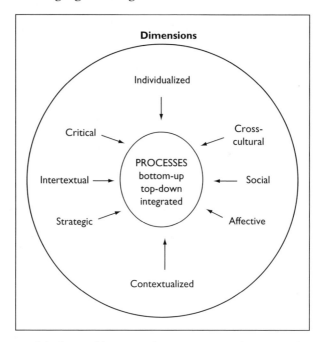

Figure 7.1 Model of second language listening comprehension (Flowerdew and Miller 2005: 86)

The model is intended to reflect (and encourage) the full range of listening skills. Working clockwise from the top of the diagram, it allows for individual variation in interpreting input and emphasizes that teachers and materials writers need to be sensitive to individual learning styles and the needs of specific learner groups. The model recognizes that learners from different cultures bring different schemata to a listening activity. It highlights the importance of participatory listening in conversation as a social activity and the way that a listening task can be constructed to set up a number of different listener roles. The model reminds us of the influence of affect—attitude, motivation, emotions, and physical feelings—on listening; for example, listening to a live speech is likely to create a different level of engagement and attention than listening to the same speech on a DVD or in an audio file. The contextual dimension is a reminder that any real-life listening event arises within a physical and cognitive context. For example, university students attending a lecture may have prepared themselves for listening by doing assigned readings or attending previous lectures; they may be working with a lecture handout or following PowerPoint slides and producing their own notes; they may be listening with a view to future selective use of the lecture content in later assignments or examinations. The model acknowledges the need to include strategy development in a second language listening programme, in particular, metacognitive strategies. It reflects the growing interest in the intertextual nature of language use and comprehension—'how any utterance is likely to reflect the past linguistic experience of speaker and hearer' (Flowerdew and Miller 2005: 93)—which is evident, for instance, in people's everyday use of catchphrases from television programmes and slogans from advertisements. Finally, the critical component of the model encourages teachers to help learners to recognize that all texts are products of their historical and sociopolitical setting and to 'deconstruct' a text to identify the speaker's assumptions and prejudices—for instance, noticing that the automation expert in the extract from O'Neill and Scott (1974) chose to refer to the factory workers as 'girls'. In short, the checklist provides us with a good basis for varying the scope and focus of our listening tasks.

Designing listening materials

In this section I consider two key issues in choosing or creating listening materials (input and/or tasks): their likely difficulty for second language listeners, and their authenticity.

Difficulty

Gary Buck's book on the assessment of listening (Buck 2001) provides a very helpful summary of the features of listening input and task that can cause second language learners' problems. These are shown in Table 7.3.

How we deal with these potential sources of difficulty depends partly on whether we are selecting listening texts or developing our own from scratch. Most teachers are more likely to be looking out for listening materials—on the radio, television, or Internet—that are suitable for a particular group of students, rather than to be designing a complete listening course. When we find a listening text that is thematically suitable, but linguistically too difficult, for those learners, some form of grading may make it more accessible. Grading has conventionally been based on two broad options: grade the text or grade the task.

The text can be made easier by adjusting either the input itself or the accompanying material. In the case of the input, it can be **pre-modified** (by preparing a script that restricts the number of unfamiliar items) or **post-modified** (by editing out faster or more complex passages). Grading by means of adjusting the accompanying materials could take the form of a list of vocabulary—which could be studied in a pre-listening activity—or a summary, or a partial transcript. The task can be graded in terms of either *process* or *output*. Process equates to the learners' listening purpose: whether they are required, for instance, to identify key points, the current topic of conversation, or a speaker's accent. Output can be graded by means of the physical outcome—what the learners have to produce as evidence of comprehension: a non-verbal response such as matching or ticking, or answering questions in their first

Input characteristics
Language
• speech rate
• lack of pauses between idea units
• unfamiliar accent
• use of less frequent vocabulary
• grammatical complexity
• embedded idea units
• complex pronoun reference.

Explicitness
• implicit ideas
• lack of redundancy.

Organization
• events narrated out of natural time order
• examples preceding the point they illustrate.

Content
• unfamiliar topics
• number of things and people referred to
• unclear indication of the importance of protagonists in the text
• shifting relationships between protagonists
• abstract content.

Context
• lack of visual or other support.

Task characteristics
Tasks tend to be more difficult when they require:
• the processing of more details
• the integration of information from different parts of the text
• the recall of gist (for example, writing a summary) rather than exact content
• the separation of fact from opinion
• the recall of non-central or irrelevant details
• a delayed response rather than an immediate one.

Table 7.3 Sources of difficulty in second language listening (adapted from Buck 2001: 149–51)

language, would be easier than having to write a summary or to answer in the second language.

However, both text-based and task-based grading have their disadvantages. Grading the text raises complex issues of assessing the level of vocabulary. A particular item in a text may be relatively uncommon—such as the expression 'flirting with the coast' in the weather forecast in the Introductory task—but its meaning may be easy to infer from context. So it is hard to predict which words and expressions will be problematic in a specific listening text. Grading aspects of the task can lead to a conflict between what the teacher or materials writer expects of the students and what they expect of themselves.

I have found that elementary-level learners—including myself, most recently in Spanish—may get frustrated when they are able to answer what they think is an over-simple question, such as saying how many speakers are taking part in a conversation, which can be done without having understood anything of the message.

Authenticity

The issue of authenticity of second language materials and tasks has been debated by applied linguists and methodologists for at least the last three decades, and even its definition has been disputed. The definition widely accepted in the language teaching profession in the 1970s and 1980s was that authentic texts were samples of language being used for real communication between native speakers, and not specifically recorded for language teaching purposes. By that narrow definition the very natural-sounding recordings featured in ground-breaking listening courses such as *Advanced Conversational English* (Crystal and Davy 1975) and *Listen to This!* (Underwood 1971) would have to be categorized as inauthentic, since they were recorded solely with pedagogic use in mind. But, in the light of the growing interest in the role of English for international communication, often between second language users, the old 'natives only' definition can no longer be sustained. It would be difficult to claim, for example, that BBC World Service documentaries, speeches in English at the United Nations, and CNN news programmes are not authentic simply because the intended audience is made up predominantly of non-native listeners.

Early in the professional debate over authenticity Henry Widdowson proposed a separation of two different aspects of language in use: 'genuineness' and 'authenticity' (Widdowson 1979). He argued that a text was genuine if it contained the sort of language typical of that genre in actual use, and that it did not matter (for learners or teachers) whether it had occurred in real communication. The term 'authentic', on the other hand, he reserved for the appropriacy of the response from the listener or reader. In other words, genuineness was related to text; authenticity was related to task. A text could be genuine even if it had been 'invented' for teaching purposes rather than 'discovered' in actual use. The UK weather forecast shown in the Introductory task for this chapter is genuine, in that its language is typical of that currently used by BBC Radio 4 UK weather forecasters; I believe it is not possible to decide whether I invented or discovered it. (In fact, I invented it.)

Recently Jack Richards criticized what he called the 'myth' of authenticity (Richards 2007). Echoing Henry Widdowson's article of 30 years ago, he argued that it is neither realistic nor necessary to base second language instruction on 'authentic' texts. In the specific case of listening materials, he pointed out that authentic texts are in fact largely unusable, given the logistical difficulties of recording conversations, as well as the issue of copyright and the ethical problem of getting informed consent of the participants. So we can think of authenticity (in its Widdowsonian sense) as the goal or aim of language teaching: teachers should bring learners to the point where they can understand, interpret, and respond to second language listening input in the way that the original speaker intended. We should not be over-concerned with finding real texts; realistic texts will do just as well, provided they are used in a way that helps learners to respond to them appropriately.

Video materials: selection and use

At various points in this book I have alluded to the importance of including video materials and video-based activities in the second language learners' diet of listening. Table 1.1 emphasized how the different media of print, audio, and video complement each other; in Chapter 2 I referred to Philip Riley's analysis of the vital functions of visual cues in understanding spoken language; and in Chapter 6 I cited David Mendelsohn's proposal that listening strategy instruction should use primarily video materials. The fundamental point is that video materials reflect the learners' likely encounters with the second language: 'learners should be exposed when possible to input that is multimodal, thus restoring some ecological validity to the learning experience' (Guichon and McLornan 2008: 91). However, the relative wealth of the information available to the learner watching video material (as opposed to listening to audio) needs to be carefully managed in classroom activities, and I find it helpful to use the Design menu shown in Table 7.4 when I am planning activities exploiting video material.

Design example: 'How does glue work?'

In this section I work through a practical example of decisions taken in designing listening activities based on a one-way video listening text. (In Chapter 9 I will give an example of two-way listening task design.) Some years ago I was looking for suitable video materials for international students from a variety of disciplines. As part of International Science Week in 1997, Channel 4 had broadcast a series of three-minute talks given by eminent scientists, who were asked to talk about topics over which there was uncertainty or disagreement; for this reason the series was entitled *Black Holes of Science*. The one that seemed to lend itself best to classroom exploitation was 'How does glue work?' by Professor Richard Gregory of the University of Bristol. A transcript of his talk, with details of accompanying visual information where it was relevant to the spoken message, is given in Table 7.5.

I decided to use the video in two ways: for listening comprehension and post-listening language study. Below are sections of the student worksheet, followed in each case by the rationale for my design decisions.

Design menu

GENERAL DECISIONS

Quantity	How much (little) should I use?
Focus	What (visual) aspects of the material seem worth exploiting?
Mode	Which hardware facilities might be used?
Type	What sort of task does the material lend itself to?
Integration	How can I link it with other language skills and activities?

DETAILED DECISIONS

Focus	language spoken
	body language (facial expressions, gestures)
	speakers' actions
	background
Mode	normal (continuous) playthrough
	interrupted playthrough
	sound only
	image only
	picture search (speeded viewing)
	freeze frame
Type	watch and do (for example, labelling a diagram)
	watch and respond (for example, which character do you sympathize with?)
	watch and answer (factual questions)
	watch and compare (for example, transcript and speech)
	watch and predict (how will this end? what will she say next?)
	watch and retell (take notes for an oral summary of what happened)
	watch and discuss (opinion exchange on basis of text content)
	watch and evaluate (what do you think of the views expressed?)

Table 7.4 Design menu

How does glue work?

ACTIVITY 1 Pre-viewing

Today's talk is by Professor Richard Gregory of Bristol University, on the subject of glue. In the space below, write a definition of glue, and then your explanation of how it works.

Definition: Glue is …

Explanation: What makes glue work is …

Actions	Words
Professor Gregory appears in a tight head-and-shoulders shot.	Something that puzzles me is glue. Why is it that one glue will stick to one thing, that thing will stick to something else, but **it won't stick to another substance or object?**
The shot widens to show he is sitting on a stool with a frying pan on his lap.	Now, I've got a non-stick frying pan here. **Why doesn't that stick to food?** How does a non-stick surface stick to the pan? There's obviously a glue that does stick to a non-stick surface.
He holds up the pan and shows a small block of wood and a tube of glue.	
He squeezes glue on to the block of wood and presses the block on to the surface of the pan.	Now, what happens if I take an ordinary glue and a bit of wood, and **I'm going to put some glue on it** and this is an experiment—I don't know the answer to this myself.
He taps the side of his head.	So I'm going to put it on the pan and **hold it for a bit and we'll see what happens**. Now, it's clear, isn't it, that there are molecular, atomic perhaps forces within an object which hold the bits of it together and when it's one object which sticks to another object with a glue there are obviously **complex forces at the atomic level** which we can't see, and I gather that they're very difficult actually to measure, these forces. So, I rather think actually that exactly how glue works **is not really known very well in science**. Whatever the case, eh, I often think that, you know, questions are the exciting things that make us live in our heads, that make us have fun talking to each other and experimenting with objects. So, **let's see what's happened** in this little experiment.
He lifts the pan and turns it upside down.	If I turn the pan upside down with the piece of wood on it what happens? It's stuck.
	Now I wonder how actually stuck that is?

Now he turns it the right way up and pushes at the block of wood.	**I'm going to give it a bit of a push**—oh! that's stuck quite well.
The wood comes away from the pan surface.	Or has it? Well, I don't really know the answer now. How much stick has there got to be before we say that glue sticks? **I don't think that's good enough for** carpentry.
He puts the wood and the tube of glue back in the pan. Smiles at the camera.	Probably one would say it's not really stuck very well. But **what would be fun would be to get lots of glues**, lots of different kinds of objects and see what sticks to what, and then you'd get the sort of relationship between objects, stick and glue, hopefully, ultimately with **an explanation of what's going on** at the atomic hidden level of the tiny minutiae of matter. Wouldn't that be fun?

Table 7.5 How does glue work?

I wanted to make sure that everyone in the class knew the word 'glue'; the Definition task in the worksheet allowed students who were familiar with it to share their information with the others, so everyone was able to draft a written definition so they could assess which one was the best expressed. The Explanation activity was meant to be challenging, since they were about to hear Professor Gregory say that precisely how glues work is something of a scientific mystery. It was also intended to set up a real purpose for listening.

ACTIVITY 2 First viewing

Watch the talk and try to identify the main ideas. Make brief notes on what you hear.

Question to the speaker: Choose something in the talk that you haven't fully understood. Formulate a question that you would ask Richard Gregory, to get clarification. Write it down in the space below.

I wanted to see how much the learners could grasp on first hearing, since that is what they were already having to do in their university lectures. The Question to the speaker would require them to compose a suitable 'local' request for clarification of the sort they might need to produce in their subject lectures.

ACTIVITY 3 Second viewing

Watch again and see whether you are able to grasp the point better the second time.
Question to other listeners: Now think of a question that you think the other students should be able to answer, having heard the talk. (It *can* be a question to which you don't know the answer yourself.) Write it out below. Ask your neighbour to answer it.

This time the learners would be listening out for the information they had focused on in their Question to the speaker, giving them the chance to see whether simple repetition of the talk would clear up their doubts. I usually build in some sort of peer comprehension question into listening classes; I will be coming back to this point in Chapter 10. In this case the Question to other listeners allows each student to choose between a display question (to which they know the answer) and a real question, which makes the answer genuinely meaningful for them.

For Stage 1 of the Post-listening section of the worksheet, the students are given a transcript of Professor Gregory's talk, with a number of phrases deleted (the phrases highlighted in bold in the transcript in Table 7.5).

ACTIVITY 4 Post-listening

Stage 1: Assimilated words: Each blank in the transcript contains some words produced with natural assimilation. Listen and try to complete them.

Check your answers with a partner. Do you agree on how many words there were in each blank?

Stage 2: Sentence signals in speech: Look back to the transcript. Which three words does Professor Gregory regularly use to mark the *start of sentences* in his talk?

Have you noticed similar expressions used by the lecturers in your department? (The teacher will collect your examples on the board.)

ACTIVITY 5 Vocabulary in speech

Stage 1: Bits and pieces: The word 'bit' is common in spoken English and has various meanings. Professor Gregory said:

'… I've got a bit of wood'

'… hold it for a bit and we'll see what happens'

'… forces which … hold the bits of it together'

'… I'm going to give it a bit of a push'

How many *different* meanings are represented in those four examples?

Write an alternative expression (to the right of each example), with the same meaning as Professor Gregory intended.

What is the Scottish expression for 'a *little* bit'? (A … bit.)

This Vocabulary in speech section was designed to get the students thinking about different meanings of a familiar word. I expected that the time meaning of the expression 'for a bit' would be unfamiliar; I have found from using this material over a number of years that in most cases it is, but that some students are able to guess its meaning from the context. Generally there will be one or two students in a class who know the Scottish adjective 'wee' and this exercise gives them the chance to show that. We go on to discuss other examples of dialect words they have picked up in Edinburgh through listening.

Suggestions for further reading

Anderson, A. and **T. Lynch.** 1988. *Listening.* Oxford: Oxford University Press. Chapters 4, 6, and 7 discuss ways of grading listening difficulty in both one-way and two-way listening tasks, with practical examples.

Flowerdew, J. and **L. Miller.** 2005. *Second Language Listening.* Cambridge: Cambridge University Press. The authors discuss materials designed within their pedagogic model for second language listening (Figure 7.1).

Rubin, J. 1995. 'The contribution of video to the development of competence in listening' in D. Mendelsohn and J. Rubin (eds.) *A Guide for the Teaching of Second Language Listening.* San Diego, CA: Dominie Press. An excellent review of why and how we should use video materials.

White, G. 1998. *Listening.* Oxford: Oxford University Press. A comprehensive and innovative collection of listening activities.

Discussion and study questions

1 Choose a listening activity from one of your second language coursebooks. Write an alternative set of questions using Nuttall's six types as a guide. Think about the questions and rank them in order of difficulty. Then try the new questions out on one of your classes. Which question do the learners find the most difficult? Does the actual order of difficulty match what you predicted?

2 Find a listening activity in a published coursebook for which you have the tapescript. Decide what you could focus on in the post-listening stage. Show the tapescript to a teaching colleague and see what language points they would choose to focus on.

3 Select some video material that you think could be of interest to one of your current classes. With a colleague, if possible, watch the material and then work through the Design menu together, comparing your decisions on how to use the material in the classroom.

8 INTEGRATING LISTENING WITH THE OTHER SKILLS

Introductory task

Do you think the classroom conversation below comes from a lesson in listening, speaking, reading, or writing?

P do you know gall bladder? gall bladder? + gall + bladder + maybe you must know + you do you know liver? + + liver

Q river

P liver in your body

Q ah liver

P liver yes + and gall bladder is near liver (*gestures*) like that

Q hmhm

P gall bladder + you know? + it's like that

Q ah

P and sometimes many patients suffer from stone in gall bladder + maybe you

T can you tell me what the gall bladder does?

P pardon?

T can you tell me what the gall bladder does?

P does?

T what is it for?

Q function

P ah ah its function is uh almost I must mention about the system of uh the solution and + + how to say + + solution and the accumulation of deposits

T hmhm

P so liver function to help + liver function to + + + help liver function to + + +

R secret

P yes secret liquid for digestion for fat

T ok that's what the liver does + now what does the gall bladder do?

P so from gall bladder some secretion go to intestine

T ok

P and it helps to dissolve lipid + and so especially after taking some lipodemic food

Q hm?

T sorry some what food?

P lipodemic
T does that mean fatty?
P ah fatty + fatty food
T sorry' cause I'm not a doctor + right + fatty food
P the gall bladder secrets some liquid to solve this food
T to dissolve it
Q ah I know
T ok

(Lynch 1996a: 143–4)

Connections

Conventionally, language teachers talk in terms of four major skills: listening, speaking, reading, and writing. Most materials designers also express their syllabuses in those terms and many course timetables name lessons after a single skill. However, it would be difficult to claim that the four skills actually function as separate entities. The lesson from which the Introductory task extract came was, according to the course timetable, a lesson in academic writing. The students were asked to find out about the background knowledge of their peers, prior to writing a definition of a technical term from their own academic field for readers from other disciplines. Student P had decided to define the term 'laparoscopic cholecystectomy'—removal of the gall bladder by keyhole surgery—and so began by checking whether her three listeners (Q, R, and T) knew the English word 'gall bladder'. So this was a pre-writing task requiring detailed listening and speaking.

Listening is a prime example of integration, in a number of ways. Firstly, it engages the clusters of sub-skills necessary for recognition, interpretation, and participation (shown in Table 3.1). Secondly, effective listening also relies on integrated application of the learner's phonological, lexical, and grammatical knowledge of the second language (McDonough 1976). Thirdly, listening relies on the integration of non-linguistic resources, such as content and formal schemata, and contextual knowledge. Finally, listening occurs in combination with the other three conventional language skills:

> Only in certain circumstances—for instance in a lecture, at the theater, or when listening to the radio—does listening appear to be an isolated skill, not interacting with other language skills. (Oxford 1996: 206)

In this section I consider the real-life interconnections between listening and reading, listening and speaking, and listening and viewing, before moving on to discuss practical classroom activities that encourage the use of integrated skills.

Listening/reading

To claim that the two modes of comprehension, listening and reading, are identical would be extreme. Physically, the decoding aspect of comprehension is clearly different between the two, requiring the processing of sound in one case and of print or handwriting in the other. But researchers have been interested in the extent of the possible overlap between the two modes, both in first and second languages. First language research suggests that age is a key variable in the relative dominance or strength of the two skills. Among children of primary school age, who are still learning to read, listening has been found to be a more efficient channel (as measured through tests of text recall), but by the time children begin secondary education, reading is the more effective comprehension mode (Sticht and James 1984). Other studies, which have found no measurable difference between reading and listening performance, have nevertheless established that listeners rely more on schematic, top-down processing than readers do, and that they also produce more idiosyncratic responses and a better grasp of implied ideas, as discussed in Chapter 4.

For our purposes, the key question is how this relates to second language learners, who—since they are mainly non-fluent processors of the target language—might encounter unique decoding difficulties in both modes. Randall Lund's study of American students of German at Brigham University (Lund 1991) found that at elementary and intermediate levels, readers were able to recall more information than listeners, but there was no difference at the advanced level. However, listeners at all three levels recalled a higher proportion of main ideas from the text than did their reading counterparts. Randall Lund concluded that the general processes underlying the two comprehension modes must be similar, and he proposed a classroom method for combining second language listening and reading in three 'passes'. Learners would first listen to a passage to grasp its overall point; they would then read a transcript, to give them access to the linguistic form; and finally they would listen again. He argued that listening should be the first and final experience of the second language text; if the first experience were that of reading the written form, learners would have unhelpfully full access to the language of the passage, and would not need to listen with such attention.

Listening/speaking

The idea of reducing the separation between these two skills by referring to two-way listening as 'listening/speaking' came from Robert Oprandy of Columbia University, New York. He believed that the conventional division into four language skill areas had served its purpose, as an 'organizational convenience', but was no longer justified, in the light of what is known about the symbiosis between listening and speaking as 'two networks within the much bigger communicative whole' (Oprandy 1994: 153). Similarly, in a review of the methodology of second language listening skills instruction, Jens Bahns identified the growing appreciation of the importance of interactive listening as a defining characteristic of 1990s thinking and practice:

> as the main aim of teaching listening is to prepare the students for real-life social interaction, it is imperative that developing listening is seen in combination with developing speaking. (Bahns 1995: 537)

I have summarized the reasons for connecting listening and speaking in terms of three research-based principles (Lynch 1996b). Principle 1 was: Listeners make better speakers. The evidence from a Scottish study of the first language listening/speaking of secondary pupils in transactional paired communication tasks was that what helped them to perform more effectively as speakers was not, as one might suppose, previous practice in the speaking role, but previous experience as the listener in a pair (Brown, Anderson, Shillcock, and Yule 1984). Principle 2 was: Listeners affect what speakers say. Successful speaking in face-to-face interaction requires adjusting to the listener's level, in terms of both their linguistic and background knowledge. Principle 3—Conversation involves listening and speaking—encapsulated what we have seen in Chapter 5 of this book: that the roles of listener and speaker alternate in real conversation. If they did not, it would not be a conversation. So conversational listeners have a vital speaking role, providing verbal and other feedback on successful understanding of what is being said, and conversational speakers have to be alert listeners, both to monitor what they are saying themselves and what the other person is saying, including the 'listener feedback' on comprehensibility.

Listening/viewing

In Chapter 2 I referred to Philip Riley's analysis of the role of the visual element in listening comprehension and his five types of visual cue: 'deictic', 'interactional', 'modal', 'indexical', and 'linguistic'. Susan Kellerman of the University of York supported his contention that the role of the visual tends to be underestimated, pointing out that in both language teaching and speech perception research there had been a tacit assumption that listening is solely dependent on hearing (Kellerman 1990). Yet there was strong evidence that the visual cues available in face-to-face, or face-to-screen, listening directly influence what we perceive. This had been demonstrated in a study by McGurk and MacDonald (1976), who showed a film of a speaker making the lip movements for the syllable [ga] to a group of adult native speakers of English. Dubbed on to the soundtrack was the syllable [ba]. Virtually all (98 per cent) of the listeners reported hearing the sound [da]. The reason for this illusion, now known as the McGurk effect, is that a speaker's lip movements for [ga] are also consistent with the lip setting for [da], but are incompatible with [ba]. This striking finding underlines the importance—and occasional predominance—of what we see for what (we think) we hear.

A recent study set out to measure the effects of different visual elements on second language listening comprehension. Sueyoshi Ayano and Debra Hardison of Michigan State University compared the relative importance of gestures and facial cues in the comprehension scores achieved by 42 low-intermediate and advanced learners of English at Michigan State University, who were played a recording of a native speaker lecture (Ayano and Hardison 2005). Some of the learners listened to an audio-only version; others watched a video showing only the lecturer's face; and a third group watched a video showing both the lecturers' facial expressions and gestures. The participants' scores on a multiple-choice test of content comprehension showed that at both levels of English proficiency the video versions were better understood than the audio only. Among the advanced learners, the face-only version produced the highest scores, while for the low-intermediate listeners the video version showing both facial expressions and gestures was the best understood. Questionnaire responses also revealed the listeners' positive appreciation of visual cues in listening. These findings provide useful empirical support for the calls by methodologists such as David Mendelsohn and Joan Rubin that teachers should be aiming to help learners make effective use of the visual dimension in 'listening' classes, especially at lower levels of second language proficiency.

Integrating listening and speaking: free talk

Conversation is the spoken genre that most clearly combines listening and speaking without either reading or writing. Although such listening/speaking is common in real life, it is relatively rare in the second language classroom—indeed, it has even been claimed that, since conversation is spontaneous interaction, by definition it cannot occur in the classroom, where all interaction has a planned pedagogic purpose (Seedhouse 1996). However, with international students at the University of Edinburgh I use an activity that I call **free talk**, which is designed to encourage them to engage in spontaneous discussion which I think comes close to 'conversation', even in a classroom setting. See what you think.

The starting point for free talk is my assumption that every student coming to a speaking class is interested in *something* and that the teacher's job is to find a way of giving them the chance to talk about whatever that something is. I leave the choice of topics entirely to the students, and there are no materials prepared in advance. In Stage 1, at the start of the lesson, I ask the students to write down on a sheet of paper a question they want an answer to, or a problem they need a solution to. There is no restriction on the type of question; it could be anything from a language question, such as 'What's the difference between "make" and "do"?', to the meaning of life—in fact, a Greek student took the opportunity to ask 'Why are we here?'. The only criterion is that each person's topic must be something to which they are genuinely interested in hearing an answer or a solution.

Stage 2 begins once everyone has completed their sheet. They form groups of three or four and work in parallel for 45 minutes or so, discussing the questions raised by their partners. As they talk, I move from group to group, monitoring what they are saying. I make notes of anything I think will be worth commenting on at the feedback stage—particularly points that I notice have caused communication breakdowns. If a learner asks me for help during the group work over a problem of self-expression, I give it, but as far as possible I try not to allow my response to turn into an extended teaching episode. The final part of the lesson (Stage 3) is set aside for comments on their discussion. First, I ask the learners themselves to report on points they remembered having had difficulty with, either in listening or speaking. Then I select and comment on some of the language points noted during group work.

My experience of using free talk with mixed groups of international graduates over the past 15 years or so is that it 'works', in two ways. Firstly, it encourages keen participation and generates real communication on topics nominated by the students themselves. Secondly, the interactions that the groups co-construct display many of the features of spontaneous conversation: changes of direction, digressions, and—notably—laughter. You have already read an extract from a free talk lesson—Isabel's anecdote about Seville oranges in Chapter 6. In the episode below the topic has moved on to Yuko's recent trip to Spain.

ISABEL	so where did you stay in Seville?
YUKO	uh in + the centre of Seville + + judisch + the place where +
ISABEL	Barrio Santa Cruz?
YUKO	yes that's right
ISABEL	(*laughs*)
YUKO	that's right (*to Khalid*) there are a lot of + small paths + in Santa Cruz

ISABEL	uh-huh yeah
YUKO	many people lose their way
ISABEL	yeah? I believe that + it's not so easy
YUKO	no
ISABEL	it's very funny but + last Christmas + this Christmas some friends of mine I mean seven + Singaporean people came to Seville and they stayed also in the Barrio Santa Cruz
YUKO	hm
ISABEL	so it must be very popular place to stay + or something + I don't know + because
YUKO	hm
ISABEL	yeah + + but it was very strange because it was raining all the time wasn't it?
YUKO	unfortunately
ISABEL	but I can tell you + that never ever happened + it had been ten years without raining + + you know + and now
YUKO	it's unusual
ISABEL	yes very unusual + yesterday I had a letter from my dad and he told me that + he said that he didn't have classes because his school was completely flooded
YUKO	flood? flooded?
ISABEL	full of water
YUKO	ah full of water?
ISABEL	yeah
YUKO	ah
KHALID	but in your place? in Seville?
ISABEL	in Seville yeah + + but it doesn't have rainy season
YUKO	it was a serious problem
ISABEL	yes so when I arrived I don't know if it was when you arrived + they didn't have water the whole day just + for twelve hours or something like this + and now floods
KHALID	floods hm + +
YUKO	and you can see a lot of orange trees
ISABEL	oh yes
YUKO	all over
KHALID	in the city in + Seville?
ISABEL	on the streets
KHALID	in Seville?
YUKO	not only in Seville + but
ISABEL	but also in Cordoba
YUKO	also in Cordoba + (*to Khalid*) Andalucian city
ISABEL	and did you try the oranges? + + did you try them?
YUKO	of course I did !
ISABEL	(*laughs*) they're very bitter aren't they?
YUKO	I like bitter

(author's classroom data 1997)

What strikes me in particular about that interaction is the way in which listening and speaking are continually interwoven, in the form of listeners' feedback to the speaker, and the way in which Yuko and Isabel, who know more about Spain, occasionally offer Khalid sociocultural information that they think he may not share, to bring him in to the conversation—even, at one point, using the expression 'rainy season' to accommodate to Khalid's Malaysian background.

Integrating listening, speaking, and writing: the Speaking Log

The 'Speaking Log' is designed to help second language learners to analyse a recording of their own spoken output and to get feedback on it from others (Lynch 2009a). It can be used with a recording of any type of speaking task, and involves learners in listening again to what they said, writing down parts that they think are incorrect or have doubts about, and then speaking to their teacher (or other learners) once the log has been completed. The log itself is very simple: a sheet of paper, divided into three columns headed 'Slips', 'Queries', and 'Teacher's comments'. It is designed for use in self-access mode and is accompanied by a set of step-by-step instructions, as shown below.

Slips	Queries	Teacher's comments

How to use the Speaking Log
There are two columns for you to fill in as you listen to your recording: *Slips* and *Queries*.

Slips
Slips are mistakes that you notice as you listen again, without anybody having to tell you. Write in the Slips column both <u>what was wrong</u> and also the <u>correct version</u>.

Queries
When you're not sure that a word or expression is correct, or if you think there must be a better way of saying it, then ask the teacher a question about it in the Queries column.

Teacher's comments
Leave this column blank for the tutor to write in their answers to your queries.

Using the feedback
When you get the log back, study the teacher's notes and comments carefully. When you get the chance, ask about anything that is not clear.

Later, try to use the language items and advice in the column next time you speak English.

(Lynch 2009a)

The Speaking Log allows students to 'listen again'—to revisit their original attempt at communication and to 'reprocess' their output (Swain and Lapkin 1995). Doing so—free of the original pressure to communicate in real time—allows them to devote more attention to what they said, and therefore to notice and note down any slips in their English. They pass the completed log to the teacher, or to another learner, who uses the Teacher's comments column to confirm (or not) the corrections of Slips and to respond to the Queries. The peer/teacher and student can then discuss the log prior to a follow-up performance.

As well as practising the skills of speaking, listening, and writing, the log integrates three different sources of feedback on their second language speech—self-, peer, and teacher—and does so with relatively basic technology. The log procedure can be adapted by teachers working with access to more advanced facilities. My students work with audio cassettes, but the log could easily be used with digital recordings, and learners who can record themselves on a mobile phone or MP3 device would have the advantage of more portable and convenient replay than with a cassette.

Integrating listening, writing, reading, and speaking: once-only dictation

A conventional way of combining all four skills is by using some form of dictation. Although it has tended to be thought of as a testing tool— which I will be coming back to in Chapter 9—dictation has become more widely used as a teaching technique in second language teaching in a wide variety of forms, in particular in the variant called 'Grammar Dictation' or **dictogloss** (Wajnryb 1990). Although dictation used to be criticized in some quarters for being a comparatively mechanical and low-level listening task, requiring reproduction rather than interpretation, the alternative view is that it usefully integrates different second language components.

One of dictation's leading advocates was John Oller of the University of California at Los Angeles, who supported the use of dictation (for testing purposes) as a means of checking learners' general proficiency in the second language, arguing that it samples what he called their **expectancy**

grammar—their underlying ability to process the second language (Oller 1979). Ironically, the same feature that led some testing researchers to object to dictation as an 'impure' test of listening—the fact that the learners need to rely on lexical and grammatical knowledge—also makes it a convenient means of integrating language skills in the classroom. Gary Buck includes various forms of dictation other than the traditional format and argues that for dictation to be useful it should reflect real-life listening needs, using spoken-style texts and challenging short-term memory, with a mixture of shorter and longer utterances (Buck 2001). Below is an example of a spoken-style text that I have used for dictation, with Gary Buck's recommendations in mind.

1 it was the day of the jungle cup final
2 and the elephants were playing the insects
3 it came to kick-off time and only ten insects were on the pitch
4 so the elephant captain said to the insect captain, 'where's number eleven?'
5 'never mind him,' said the insect captain, 'we're ok to start'
6 well the elephants were really too good for the insects
7 and by half-time they were beating the insects by two goals to nil
8 after the break out came the insects with all eleven players
9 their new player was a millipede
10 who was too quick and skilful for the elephants
11 he scored a hat-trick and the insects went on to win four two
12 as they were shaking hands the elephants' captain said to the insects' captain
13 'that millipede's brilliant, but why didn't he play from the start?'
14 'the snag is it takes him an hour to put all his boots on'

As you will see, the text includes features typical of unscripted narrative, such as informal vocabulary ('never mind him', 'snag'), utterances of varying lengths to challenge working memory, and natural repetition (the recurrences of 'captain'). I use the 'cup final' text as a once-only dictation—in other words, I read the script only once, initially pausing for 25–30 seconds after each of the 14 lines for the learners to write down what they have heard. Working in pairs, they then compare their versions and discuss which is better. In cases where only one of them has attempted a particular word, they can discuss whether it seems plausible. After 10–15 minutes of pair work I read through the whole text once again, at normal speed, for the students to confirm or change what they discussed after the first hearing. In the feedback phase, I usually focus class discussion on to two areas: points that they 'heard' the second time but not the first; and points that they heard first time but changed after the second hearing.

Suggestions for further reading

Lynch, T. 1983. 'A programme to develop the integration of comprehension skills.' *ELT Journal* 37/1: 58–61. Description of a series of comprehension lessons integrating listening and reading.

White, G. 1998. *Listening.* Oxford: Oxford University Press. Chapter 7 provides detailed instructions for seven projects combining listening with other skills.

Discussion and study questions

1 Paul Seedhouse claims that conversation—spontaneous, non-directed talk with equal opportunities for listeners to speak—is not possible in a second language lesson. Do you agree? Is there any point in letting learners 'just talk'?

2 If you wanted to find out whether individual students in a second language class were better at reading or listening, how would you do it? Discuss this with teaching colleagues. If possible, plan and carry out an assessment of the two skills in one of your classes.

3 If you wanted to design an activity in which your students listen to and read a text at the same time, do you think it would be better to provide an exact transcript of what they hear, or a transcript in which there are some acceptable differences between the spoken and written version, or a transcript with mistakes in it? How would the listening activities be different?

9 ASSESSMENT OF LISTENING COMPREHENSION

Introductory task

Below is my recollection of a true story about 'Boris', a Russian immigrant to Canada, which David Mendelsohn told in his plenary talk at the 1992 TESOL Convention. What does it tell us about the assessment of listening?

> Boris enrolled in one of David Mendelsohn's ESL classes at York University in Toronto. He had left his family in Russia and was working as a taxi driver. During the first lesson Boris seemed ill at ease in the listening activities. At the end of the lesson he came up to David Mendelsohn and the following exchange (as I remember it) took place:
>
> BORIS   Why Canadians not speak correct English? I not understand people here.
> DAVID   What makes you think we don't speak correctly?
> BORIS   Canadians speak English different from English I study in Russia. Is not correct.
> DAVID   Well, don't forget you arrived only recently. As you get more listening practice, I'm sure you'll find you understand us more.
> BORIS   No. Problem is Canadians. They must speak correct English.
>
> The classes and the months passed. At first Boris continued to complain about the substandard quality of Canadian speech, but in time his complaints lessened. Within a year he had made enough progress in English to leave the ESL class and had saved enough money to bring his family to join him in Toronto. When his wife 'Olga' arrived, she enrolled in the same class that Boris had attended the year before. During the first lesson, Olga was showing similar signs of unease in listening activities and at the end of the lesson she waited behind to speak to David Mendelsohn. At that point, Boris arrived to collect Olga and came into the classroom to say hello. The conversation then continued along these lines:
>
> OLGA   I not understand people here. Why Canadians not speak correct English?
> DAVID   (*with a sense of déjà vu*) What makes you think we don't speak correctly?
> BORIS   Olga, if you think Canadians' English is very bad now, you should have been here last year. Last year it was *much* worse.

Problems of listening assessment

As the Boris example shows, it can be difficult to monitor improvements in our own listening ability in another language, and if it is hard for us to be aware of changes when we have such privileged access, it is that much more problematic for researchers and teachers to assess the listening performance of language learners. In the mid-1990s one of the leading specialists in listening comprehension testing, Irene Thompson of George Washington University, sounded a warning about the lack of research to provide second language teachers with helpful support in creating listening tests:

> While there has been some research in testing of L2 reading comprehension, relatively little has been done with the assessment of listening...With little systematic and principled research to guide them, language teachers are largely left to their own devices when it comes to developing listening comprehension tests. (Thompson 1995: 31)

In the 15 years since the publication of Thompson's review, a number of testing studies have helped to improve our understanding of what makes second language listening effective and therefore what we should be aiming to assess in our students' listening repertoire (e.g. Buck and Tatsuoka 1998; Freedle and Kostin 1999; Buck 2001). Gary Buck and Kikumi Tatsuoka of the Educational Testing Service applied a sophisticated statistical procedure, the rule-space technique, to language testing for the first time (Buck and Tatsuoka 1998). It is normally used to break test items down into cognitive attributes that represent the underlying knowledge and skills that the items measure, and then analyses each candidate's pattern of responses to calculate an individual's chances of having mastered each attribute. The research involved a listening comprehension test taken by 412 Japanese college students, involving five passages arranged in order of increasing difficulty. Statistical analysis of the students' answers showed that 15 attributes accounted for virtually all the variance in their performances. These were the abilities to:

– recognize the task by deciding what constitutes task-relevant information
– scan fast spoken text automatically and in real time
– process a substantial information load
– process dense information
– use previous items to locate information
– identify relevant information without explicit markers
– understand and make use of marked word stress
– make text-based inferences
– incorporate background knowledge into text processing
– process second language concepts with no literal first language equivalent
– recognize and exploit redundancy
– process information scattered throughout a text
– construct a response quickly and efficiently.

The overall conclusion that Gary Buck and Kikumi Tatsuoka drew stressed—once more—the immense complexity of the processes involved in listening: 'second-language listening ability is not a point on one linear continuum, but a point in a multi-dimensional space, and the number of dimensions is large' (Buck and Tatsuoka 1998: 146). Amidst this complexity there are three main obstacles to assessing second language learners' listening skills, which I will briefly discuss: the inaccessibility of mental processes, the difficulty of isolating listening skills from the other language skills and other types of knowledge, and test anxiety.

Inaccessibility of listening processes

Even with the most recent advances in brain imaging technology, which allows neuroscientists to track the sites of brain activity while a person is listening, it is still impossible for the observer to see the listener's thoughts. So we are forced to find ways of assessing listening by 'equating it with behaviours that can be monitored directly and quantified, such as questions answered, propositions recalled, or pictures identified correctly' (Thompson 1995: 31). However, it is not easy to design listening comprehension tests that reflect the purposes of real-life listening, partly because most routine listening tasks require either little or no response from the listener, other than—in the case of interactive listening—the use of acknowledgement tokens such as 'uh-huh' and 'oh?'. As Geoff Brindley has pointed out, very few of us are likely to find ourselves needing in real life to match incoming speech against alternative written options (as in multiple-choice item tests), or to absorb and reproduce detailed information without being able to make notes—yet both these forms of assessment are common in second language listening tests (Brindley 1998). Apart from the fact that tests involve comparatively unnatural tasks, the listening test designer faces the problem of the inevitable indirectness of the act of assessment, which Bernard Spolsky summed up in the following way:

SPEAKER 1	encodes information in
TEXT 1	which is to be comprehended by
LISTENER 1	the candidate, who understands it (in the light of background knowledge, second language knowledge, context, sense of purpose, etc.) and becomes
READER 1	who reads and interprets
TEXT 2	the listening test questions, composed by
WRITER 1	the test designer, to become
WRITER 2	(the candidate) responding to those questions by producing
TEXT 3	the answers, which are to be interpreted and marked by
READER 2	the examiner, who in turn becomes
WRITER 3	by producing
TEXT 4	the candidate's mark or score, which has to be interpreted by
READER 3	the test user

(adapted from Spolsky 1994: 147)

Given the length of that chain of interpretation, 'it is not hard to recognise that Text 4 produced in this way may have only a partial relationship to our original concern, Listener 1's understanding of Text 1' (Spolsky 1994: 148).

Isolating the listening component

Chapters 3–5 explored the potential range of internal and external resources—knowledge of the world, of language and of culture, first-hand experience, emotions, and intelligence—that a listener may draw on. Listening can only work as smoothly as it generally does by being 'massively interactive and parallel' (Buck 1990: 409). From the point of view of assessment, this makes it extremely hard to differentiate between different levels of processing, or to ascribe success on a listening test item to the effective use of a specific listening skill. Geoff Brindley (1998) listed some of the factors affecting test performance, shown in Table 9.1.

Given what we know about the bundle of processes and sources involved in comprehension, it is difficult to design a 'pure' test of listening, free of interference from other cognitive skills or knowledge (Thompson 1995). Paradoxically, in trying to prevent 'contamination' from individual attributes, such as memory and background knowledge, the listening test designer may

---

Nature of the listening input
speech rate
length
background
syntax
vocabulary
noise
accent
register
information density
amount of redundancy

Nature of the assessment task
amount of context provided
clarity of the instructions
availability of question preview
response required (for example, direct reference, inference)

Individual listener factors
memory
interest
background knowledge
motivation

Table 9.1 Factors in listening test performance
(adapted from Brindley 1998: 175)

actually remove the factors which, although they represent confounding variables for assessment, would be helpful resources for the listener under normal circumstances. In addition to these complexities and the difficulty of isolating what we want to test, there is the risk that aspects of the listening test other than the learners' listening skill may influence their performance. Gillian Brown and George Yule (Brown and Yule 1983a) discuss four reasons why a learner might end up giving an incorrect answer to an item in a listening test (apart from the obvious one—namely, that they have not understood the relevant part of the text). Firstly, the learner may have misunderstood the question, which is a problem of reading; secondly, they may have made a slip in their answer, which is a problem of writing; thirdly, they may not have noticed a specific detail required for a correct answer to a test item, a problem of attention; and lastly, they might have forgotten what they heard and understood, which is a problem of memory. Gillian Brown and George Yule suggest the following remedies:

— to reduce the effects of reading, keep the questions simple
— to reduce the effects of writing, minimize the amount of the second language that the learners have to produce—for example, allow them to answer in their first language, or in visual form, or in a brief second language response
— to reduce the effects of lack of attention, set the learners a realistic target when you frame the test question. Think in terms of what you would expect a competent native listener to have understood or noticed
— to reduce the memory load, use while-listening questions (not post-listening ones), or short listening texts, or break up longer texts with pauses for answering the questions.

Test anxiety

Any type of test can make people nervous, but language learning appears to cause particular anxiety, especially for adult learners, and listening tests do so more than assessments in the other skills (Vogely 1999). Among the reasons suggested for this tendency are a negative attitude to listening in general, and low self-esteem regarding one's ability in second language listening, probably aggravated by the lack of control over speed of delivery (Joiner 1986). But some practical steps can be taken to reduce stress levels among learners, such as making the test instructions clear, or allowing plenty of time for the learners to get familiar with the test format, including sample items as a preview (Brindley 1998).

There is some inconclusive evidence that careful pre-assessment training in relaxation and positive thinking can help to lower listening test anxiety and also to improve test performance. In a study involving some 80 advanced-level students of English at the University of Seville, Jane Arnold (2000) found that 81 per cent of them reported feeling more nervous about listening tests than about other forms of assessment, and that they were unanimous in believing that this affected their test performance. Using a pre-test and post-test design, Arnold measured the effect on test scores of a series of visualization sessions that had been designed to reduce anxiety about listening. The post-test results showed that the learners who had done the visualization exercises achieved higher scores than a control group who did not receive such training. Students' comments in a final questionnaire suggested that they ascribed this improvement to lower anxiety levels: 'The implication is that if students are worrying about not understanding, they are not giving their full attention to the task in hand' (Arnold 2000: 784).

Although the results of Arnold's study were positive, we should bear in mind that the relationship between listening tests and anxiety is a complex one. Two other studies with larger groups of students—American learners of Japanese (Aida 1994) and Japanese learners of English (Yo 2006)—have found that test anxiety had no measurable effect on listening performance. In other words, apprehension was not reflected in comprehension.

Assessing interactive listening

In Chapter 5 I stressed that in real-life communication, listening and speaking skills are employed in tandem, as the twin components of interactive listening in conversation; and in Chapter 8 I suggested ways of integrating listening with speaking in classroom tasks that reflect the collaborative nature of such interaction. However, as Gary Buck has noted, virtually all the work on the testing of second language listening—both research and test construction—has concentrated on one-way listening in non-interactive settings. 'The ability to perform the listener's role in an interactive, collaborative situation has generally been tested as a speaking skill, usually in interview-type assessments' (Buck 2001: 98). He argues that this has happened for reasons of convenience and economy.

One of the few researchers to have addressed the assessment of interactive listening skills is George Yule, who has worked with various colleagues on studies of

effective communication in both first and second language settings, using map-based tasks (e.g. Brown and Yule 1983a; Brown, Anderson, Shillcock, and Yule 1984; Yule and Powers 1994; Yule 1997). These map-based tasks often feature one partner who has access to correct or up-to-date information, which they have to deliver to the other partner, whose map contains inadequate or out-of-date details. They are typical of the sort of information-gap tasks commonly featured in both first and second language communication research, which are designed to allow the researcher 'privileged knowledge of the state of affairs which the speaker is trying to describe' (Brown, Anderson, Shillcock, and Yule 1984: 76–7). Over the years, a great deal of time and effort has been devoted to devising tasks art-fully constructed to *require* negotiation of meaning. However, precisely because so much emphasis has been placed on channelling learners into the negotiation of meaning, there is a risk that when assessing these interactive performances, teachers will focus on the process of negotiation, and the extent of negotiation, rather than evaluating the product achieved. To remedy this situation, George Yule and Maggie Powers (1994) developed a means of assessing the quality of the product of information-gap tasks: the Communicative Outcome (CO) system, shown in Table 9.2.

---

1 **No problem**: A problem exists but is not identified by either the sender or the receiver.

2 **Non-negotiated solutions**

    a *Unacknowledged problem*: A problem is identified by the receiver but not acknowledged by the sender.

    b *Abandon responsibility*: A problem is identified by the receiver and acknowledged by the sender, but the sender does not take responsibility for solving the problem, either by saying they will skip it, leave it, never mind it or forget it, or by telling the receiver to choose any location or path.

    c *Arbitrary solution*: A problem is identified by the receiver and acknowledged by the sender who then makes an arbitrary decision about some defining feature of the location or path. The key element here is not accuracy, but the arbitrariness of the decision which does not attempt to take the receiver's world into account or to make the receiver's world match the sender's.

3 **Negotiated solutions**

    a *Receiver's world solution*: A problem is identified and acknowledged by the sender who then tries to find out what is in the receiver's world and uses that information to instruct the receiver, based on the receiver's perspective.

    b *Sender's world solution*: A problem is identified and acknowledged by the sender who then instructs the receiver to make the receiver's world match the sender's, ignoring whatever information the receiver provides which does not fit the sender's perspective.

Table 9.2 Communicative Outcome: an assessment category system (Yule and Powers 1994: 459)

This system was designed as a research instrument, as a means of analysing and scoring recordings of learners' map-based performances, rather than a way for teachers to carry out routine assessments in real time in the classroom. It might be possible to adapt and simplify the CO system, either for teachers to use to assess their students' success in two-way listening tasks, or even for the learners themselves to assess their own performances.

Alternatives to tests

In their advice on the alternatives in language assessment, James Dean Brown and Thom Hudson divided assessments into three broad types: **selected-response** assessments, such as true/false, matching and multiple-choice; **constructed-response** assessments, including gap-filling, short-answer and performance tasks; and **personal-response** assessments like portfolios and self- or peer evaluations (Brown and Hudson 1998). The first two types can be regarded as conventional or traditional, while the third type comes under the label 'alternative'. Drawing on research into alternative forms of assessment, Brown and Hudson compiled the following set of principles put forward by advocates on alternative approaches:

- require students to perform, create, or produce something
- use real-world contexts or simulations
- make the assessment non-intrusive, by extending daily classroom activities
- base assessments on meaningful tasks
- focus on processes as well as products
- tap into higher-level thinking and problem-solving
- provide information about both the strengths and weaknesses of the students
- ensure that assessment is culturally sensitive
- employ people, not machines, to do the scoring, using human judgement
- encourage open disclosure of rating criteria
- require teachers to take on novel instructional and assessment roles.

(adapted from Brown and Hudson 1998: 654–5)

Of the alternatives currently available, two are especially appropriate for assessing progress in second language listening: self-assessment and portfolios.

Self-assessment

In her survey of second language listening assessment, Irene Thompson (1995) described self-assessment as a promising approach, but emphasized that for it to be valid it should be combined with other measures of listening comprehension, such as traditional test scores. One drawback of self-assessment is that less experienced, and therefore generally lower-level, language learners tend to agree with statements in self-report questionnaires and also

Evaluating your listening

How much of the whole lecture did you understand?
1 less than 25%
2 25–50%
3 50–75%
4 more than 75%.

Which factors caused you most difficulty?
• the subject matter
• the technical vocabulary
• the speed of speaking
• the length of the spoken sentences
• the lecturer's accent
• lack of concentration.
Were there any other factors?

Evaluating your notes

How many of the main points do you think you have included in your notes?
1 all
2 most
3 some
4 none

Do your notes show
1 less than you actually understood?
2 as much as you understood?
3 more than you understood?
Compare your notes with your neighbour's. Whose notes are better? In what ways are they better?

Table 9.3 Evaluating your listening (adapted from Lynch 2004: 82)

to overestimate their language proficiency. However, she argued that these weaknesses can be reduced by various practical steps—avoiding generalized statements in questionnaires, focusing on familiar listening situations, avoiding negatively worded questions, and asking several questions on the same area. Table 9.3 shows an example of a self-assessment exercise from a listening coursebook.

Portfolios

As the name suggests, a portfolio is a collection of samples of a learner's work in listening. James Dean Brown and Thom Hudson discuss three overall advantages claimed for portfolios in the assessment literature: that they strengthen students' learning, enhance the teacher's role, and improve the breadth of the assessment process. Among the possible items for inclusion in a second language listening portfolio, Irene Thompson recommended a weekly record

Segment viewed	Student's comments	Teacher's comments
1 Young people meet on a beach.	The pre-listening activities helped me anticipate what was said. The visuals were also helpful, but sometimes I watched the actors and forgot to listen.	You could have watched the segment first with the sound off. This would have given you the 'big picture'. Then, when you watched it with the sound on, you might not have needed to attend to the visuals so much.
	There were several blanks I could not fill in. It was hard to hear what they were saying because of the music and the ocean in the background.	You could have tried figuring out what might have been said from context. What can a fellow be saying when he dives into the water after a girl he is trying to pick up?

Table 9.4 Progress card (abridged from Thompson 1995: 50)

of television programmes the learner has watched (in a self-access centre or at home), written summaries of any films they have seen, completed worksheets from listening texts selected for individual study, and progress cards (Thompson 1995: 49). Part of a sample progress card, completed by the learner and then reviewed by the teacher, is shown in Table 9.4.

Sample assessment activities

ACTIVITY 1 (ONE-WAY LISTENING)   The radio appeal

The radio appeal, in which a well-known person asks listeners to donate money to a charity, is a convenient way to assess one-way listening comprehension. To reduce the time spent preparing assessment materials, I designed the worksheet below, which can be used with any examples of this particular genre.

Radio appeal

Complete the details in the spaces below to show your understanding of what the speaker says:
Name of person making the appeal ————————————————
Name of organization needing money ————————————————
Aims ——————————————————————————————

Date founded or established _____

Statistics or figures for the work done by the organization _____

Details of any individual people mentioned _____

How money will be used _____

Specific projects _____

Address to send money to _____

Telephone number to call _____

The worksheet refers to the typical content of the radio appeal. (We will come back to this sort of generic worksheet in Chapter 10.)

ACTIVITY 2 (INTERACTIVE LISTENING) Describe and draw

Describe and draw can be used to assess learners' interactive listening in a variety of formats. The basic idea is that one person has in front of them an object, diagram, or map, which they have to describe to a partner in enough detail for them to reproduce it on paper. Since this is meant to test interactive listening, the 'listener' is encouraged (and expected) to ask for clarification when necessary. The only restriction is that the two partners must not show each other their object, diagram, or map until they believe they have completed the task successfully.

Possible formats: teacher to whole class; teacher to single learner (individual assessment); learner to learner (in pairs). Suitable sources of materials: *Teaching the Spoken Language* (Brown and Yule 1983a) and *Figures in Language* (Jordan 1982).

Suggestions for further reading

Buck, G. 2001. *Assessing Listening*. Cambridge: Cambridge University Press. The fullest account of how to assess second language listening skills.

Thompson, I. 1995. 'Assessment of second/foreign language listening comprehension' in D. Mendelsohn and J. Rubin (eds.). *A Guide to the Teaching of Second Language Listening*. San Diego, CA: Dominie Press. A concise and practical summary of a range of listening assessment types.

Discussion and study questions

1 I suggested that dictation is a suitable means of assessing one-way listening. Do you think there are any disadvantages in using it?

2 Look again at the Communicative Outcome framework for assessing performance in two-way listening tasks (Yule and Powers 1994). With a teaching colleague, try to simplify it into a form that could be used

by a teacher in class. Then try it out in your classes and compare your experiences of using it.

3 Michael Rost's listening skills framework (Table 3.1) provides a helpful analysis of what listening can involve. Take a recording of authentic speech, listen to it, refer to Table 3.1, and reflect on the skills needed in order to understand the passage fully. Compose questions that will assess whether listeners have used those skills successfully.

PART FOUR

Learning second language listening

10 LEARNER-CENTRED LISTENING

Introductory task

From the clues in this transcript, what is the relationship between Stuart and Judy?

(telephone rings)

STUART	Hello?
FIONA	Oh. Is that Stuart?
STUART	Yes.
FIONA	Hello Stuart, it's Fiona.
STUART	Oh. Hi Fiona.
FIONA	Hi. Erm...is Judy there by any chance?
STUART	No I'm sorry she's just popped out to the shops.
FIONA	Oh dear. Erm...could you possibly leave a message?
STUART	Yes. Yes. Just a second, let me get a piece...bit of paper.
FIONA	Thank you.
STUART	OK.
FIONA	Er...the thing is we've arranged to play tennis this afternoon (Mm-mm) at 3 o'clock (Yes) erm...but I've got a problem because the string on my racket's broken (Mm-mm) but I think that Judy's got an extra racquet (Yes I think she has) and so I was wondering if you could ask her to bring the extra one along.
STUART	Yes. OK. I'll do that.
FIONA	OK and...er...oh yes one other thing. She borrowed a book from me (Mm-mm) and I think she's probably forgotten all about it. I wonder if you could possibly remind her to bring that along as well.
STUART	She knows what it is, does she?
FIONA	Yes, yes. It's a novel.
STUART	Yes. OK. So bring extra racquet and...er...the book that she borrowed.
FIONA	That's right. (OK) 3 o'clock.
STUART	I'll tell her.
FIONA	Thanks very much, Stu.

STUART   OK. Cheerio.
FIONA   Bye.
STUART   Bye.

(Blundell and Stokes 1981: 35)

Later in this chapter we will see how a group of my students interpreted the relationship between Judy and Stuart.

In the classroom

Learner-centred listening

In his book on learner-centredness in second language learning, Ian Tudor wrote that

> Learner training does not ... simply involve a one-way flow of information, in which the teacher provides learners with knowledge and skills they might not possess ... It also caters for the creation of a forum within which the teacher and learners exchange insights and perceptions of the learning process and thereby initiate the shared exploration of language learning which lies at the heart of a learner-centred approach. (Tudor 1996: 37)

If I substitute the words 'listener' and 'listening' for 'learner' and 'learning', then Ian Tudor's statement encapsulates what I mean by learner-centred listening: activities in which second language listeners are encouraged to share—with each other and with the teacher—their understandings of a spoken text. The focus of attention is the exchange of individuals' reasonable interpretations, rather than the retrieval of correct answers from the text.

One way for teachers to encourage this sort of open exchange is to use examples of their own mishearings and misunderstandings. As you will have gathered from previous chapters, I keep a note of listening incidents in which I have initially failed to grasp the meaning and have only understood it after some thought. Another is to set up a two-way listening activity that I call 'Paused Listening' (Lynch 1996a). The teacher plays a recording of a narrative or a set of instructions, containing deliberate ambiguities and apparent contradictions. When any student in the class has any doubt about how to interpret what they have just heard, they call out for the teacher to pause the tape. When the teacher has pressed the pause button in response to a call of 'Stop', the learners have to agree which of four options to take:

— to have the relevant part of the recording played again
— to play on and see whether the next part resolves the ambiguity or contradiction
— to ask the teacher for additional information
— to compare their individual interpretations and see whether one seems appropriate.

Getting learners to talk through their individual 'efforts after meaning' in this way can increase their awareness of spoken language, of their internal resources for comprehension, and of ways to orchestrate those resources. Research by Christine Goh and Yusnita Taib in Singapore (2006) has shown that children as young as 11 or 12 can be guided to extend their metacognitive awareness of the listening process. Below are some of the children's comments from that study:

Notice repetitions
Take note if there are repetitions—this could mean that the point repeated is being emphasized and that it is very important.

Visualization
Picture or mental maps appear in my head when I listen to the text.

Maintain interest
If you ever encounter a passage you find boring, you still concentrate. You could connect it to something which you've experienced but not too much as that might lead to daydreaming.

Positive self-talk
Psycho myself, talk and comfort myself to get rid of negative feeling.

(Goh and Taib 2006: 229)

That 11- and 12-year-old listeners can express strategic knowledge at this level of sophistication might surprise some teachers, but it suggests we could profitably use similar techniques with older second language learners to get them thinking about their own listening processes.

Learner-generated listening activities

Now we turn to listening activities created by learners, rather than by teachers or materials writers. It is now nearly 30 years since Sidney Whitaker made his radical proposal that, since 'the standard comprehension question is inherently malignant ... the learners must ask the questions' (Whitaker 1983: 329). His argument was based on the observation that the human organism learns by interrogating its environment, seeking clues that will confirm its understanding of unfamiliar events, objects, and expressions. Language teachers, by contrast, are led by professional training and experience to be so tuned in to the notion of a single 'correct' answer that we may close our minds to perfectly reasonable alternatives. Although Sidney Whitaker was discussing comprehension questions in teaching reading, the basic principle also applies to listening: it makes more sense to get learners to ask questions about a text than to rely on those of the materials writer, because their questions will reflect their developing interpretation and their level of proficiency in the language.

In my own listening classes I extend Sidney Whitaker's proposal by combining it with Christine Nuttall's six types of comprehension question, discussed in Chapter 7. I explain to my students the differences between the question types (direct reference, inference, etc.) in order to broaden their view of what listeners can be asked to do, and to take them beyond literal and direct reference comprehension questions. I usually ask them to compose questions of three types, to get them thinking about different ways of interpreting what they have heard. One of the texts I have used for this purpose is the telephone conversation presented at the start of this chapter (Blundell and Stokes 1981). In one class, an Italian student asked the question that I asked you in the Introductory task: 'What is Stuart's relationship to Judy?' Most of the other students thought Stuart must be Judy's brother, husband, boyfriend, flatmate, or tenant. However, a Bangladeshi gave 'butler' as his answer, which intrigued his classmates because, as you will see if you look back at the transcript, there is actually very little evidence to prove that Stuart could *not* be Judy's butler. The Bangladeshi learner argued that the most plausible explanation for the presence of a man left, during the day, in a woman's home to answer calls on her behalf was that he must be doing it as paid work, and that he was therefore a domestic servant. This is a good example of the sort of culture-based interpretation discussed in Chapter 4 and a reminder that listening is the process of fitting what we hear into what we know.

One can take the idea of learner-generated listening materials a step further by asking learners themselves to select or locate a suitable text for their class and then to create listening activities to accompany it. Today's easier access to audio and video materials on the Internet makes it possible for teachers to devolve responsibility for materials selection and task creation to their students. A good example of this type of learner-directed listening materials design is the project for Spanish trainee teachers of English described by Joan-Tomàs Pujolà of the Universitat de Barcelona (Pujolà 2007). Their Cooperative Audiovisual Comprehension (CAC) project featured 'blended learning', involving conventional lecture sessions, email exchanges, and small-group tutorials as trios of learners worked on their chosen materials. The activities themselves were fairly traditional—pre-listening guessing and predicting, listening and note-taking, post-listening focus on form—but the innovative aspect of the project was the creation, sharing, and trialling of the trios' materials by their peers, making use of a variety of American, British, Canadian, and Indian texts. Although the CAC project was designed for trainee teachers, its underlying principles should be relevant to other groups of second language listeners.

In the self-access centre

Self-access centres (SACs), which arrived on a wave of enthusiasm in the 1980s, have come in for considerable criticism since then. Philip Riley of

CRAPEL, University of Nancy II, whose work broke new ground in the field of learner autonomy in the 1970s, is among those who have pointed to the limited imagination often applied to the introduction of SACs:

> Helping learners in self-access is not just a matter of telling them where they can lay their hands on such-and-such a piece of material; it also necessarily involves some degree of access to self. (Riley 1997: 116)

A recent case study by Lindsay Miller, Elza Tsang Shuk-Ching, and Mark Hopkins illustrates the importance of long-term planning, and both teacher and learner education, in setting up a reading skills SAC in a Hong Kong secondary school (Miller, Tsang, and Hopkins 2007). The authors, who acted as advisers, describe the various stages of the project's development: consulting the school's teachers in the main decision making; running a series of teacher development workshops to raise awareness of the concept of learner autonomy before moving to its realization; and, not least, involving the pupils in the equipping of the SAC, including the selection of suitable texts and the creation of worksheets to an agreed template.

Requirements for self-access listening materials

The 'self-access' dimension of SAC listening materials should not be limited to providing a transcript and answer key. If SAC listening materials are to open up the sort of learning opportunities that Philip Riley called for, they need to offer a platform for feedback (commentary, study notes, and advice on future action), as advocated by Susan Sheerin in her classic book on self-access (Sheerin 1989). One of her suggestions was that learners using a SAC should add their own questions and comments to listening worksheets for the next user of the material, to personalize the learning experience and to encourage individual involvement. SAC materials design entails considerable investment of staff time and money, but there are ways of producing listening materials at relatively low cost, of which I will mention two. The first is to create a listening activity 'template' for a particular spoken genre; the second is to encourage learners to work cooperatively in SAC listening (and speaking) activities.

Generic worksheets

Generic worksheets go by various names, such as 'standard exercises' (originally coined for reading materials by Axbey 1989), 'universal worksheets' (Kissinger 1990), and 'generic activities' (Meinhof 1998). They are based on the principle that a spoken genre displays certain defining features, which the teacher or materials designer can exploit to guide language learners' listening experience. (The radio appeal activity in Chapter 9 was an example of a generic worksheet.) Among the television genres that Ulrike Meinhof includes in her book are news programmes (with sub-categories such as

Worksheet for party political broadcasts

Content

Party: _____

Number of main speakers: _____

Aspects of party policy featured in the broadcast *(please circle them)*

Economy	Defence	Tax	Health	Industry
Education	Family	Environment	Transport	Foreign
Law and order				

Does the party leader appear? _____

Words/ideas repeated to emphasize their importance: _____

Is a party slogan used at the end? If so, write it here: _____

Does the programme include the phrase 'Vote for...'? _____

Techniques of persuasion

Which of the following are used in the broadcast?

| Film/video | Music | Statistics | Graphics | Interviews |

Are any other parties mentioned by name? Which ones? _____

Is Britain compared with any other countries? Which ones?_____

Effectiveness

What general impression of the party was the broadcast intended to create?_____

Has it changed the way you would vote? Why? _____

Table 10.1 Generic worksheet for party political television broadcasts

'political demonstration' and 'diplomatic visit'), game shows, soap operas, and advertisements. Table 10.1 shows a generic worksheet for party political television broadcasts, created by a group of advanced-level Taiwanese and Japanese learners of English studying at the University of Edinburgh during the British election year of 2004.

Collaborative SAC listening

Learners should be encouraged to think of the SAC as a place where they can work together with other learners, and not—as it is conventionally portrayed—as a site only for individual language study. Individualization need not mean segregation (Morrison 2008). There are many reasons for encouraging second language learners to work collaboratively. One is the positive effect on attention and motivation of ensuring that learners take a break from individual study, when they may have been concentrating on one activity for some time. Another is the opportunity to compare notes with someone else and to ask for help with problematic parts of the listening text. Thirdly, collaboration provides the chance to exchange their individual interpretations, in the way I have argued for.

Susan Sheerin argued that a further dimension of collaboration, though of a non-interactive sort, can be achieved by asking learners to contribute in written form to SAC listening materials—writing user reports, commenting on vocabulary they found problematic, composing content summaries of the listening text (Sheerin 1989). These are all very sensible suggestions, originally made with pen and paper application in mind; today's electronic technologies make this sort of learner contribution to the SAC materials that much more straightforward, since many will have access to database, chat room, and intranet facilities.

Linking self-access listening to learning

With the recent advances in digital technology, much of the current discussion of SAC listening focuses on multimedia applications. As yet, there is stronger evidence for the benefits of such applications in promoting short-term comprehension than longer-term learning. To take research into listeners' use of subtitles as an example, there is evidence that viewing subtitled second language video materials leads to higher comprehension scores than does use of the same material without subtitles (Price 1983). Access to second language subtitles has been found to enhance not only comprehension, but also motivation and enjoyment (Vanderplank 1988). Subtitles have also been shown to lead to increased use of new vocabulary from the video immediately after listening (Garza 1991). An interesting study of advanced English-speaking learners of Welsh as a second language reported that a translation activity in which the learners made their own first language subtitles for second language video texts brought benefits in terms of motivation (Williams and Thorne 2000). Finally, a recent study comparing the possible comprehension effects of first language and second language subtitles showed that the latter led to higher comprehension scores—presumably because reading them entails less lexical interference than reading a subtitled translation (Guichon and McLornan 2008).

Although research indicates that subtitles have led to increased comprehension, it is not clear whether that greater understanding comes from the opportunity to read the on-screen text, rather than from enhanced listening skills. If self-access multimedia materials do help develop second language listening skills in the longer term, they may do so indirectly. For example, learners using multimedia software that provides 'hot links' to sociocultural background information (of the sort found in an encyclopedia) may be helped to understand references to events and people in spoken texts they encounter in the future. Our understanding of the interaction between sound, image, on-screen text, and second language cognition is relatively limited, and arguably the safest approach to the use of multimedia in self-access listening is to be cautious (Salaberry 2001) and to involve language learners themselves in evaluating the effectiveness of combining the media in helping them to understand and learn the spoken language. As teachers, we should be wary of the calls for a 'technology-driven pedagogy' (Ibarz and Webb 2007)—a point I will come back to in the final chapter.

I am going to suggest two ways of helping second language learners to extend their knowledge and skills through post-listening noticing tasks. Both involve a focus on form and encourage learners to observe and analyse the linguistic elements in spoken texts. The first offers a set of activities that can accompany the viewing of video or DVD material; in the second, learners compare recordings of their own performance of a classroom task with those of other non-native and native speakers.

Quarrying from SAC video transcripts

In my experience, language learners tend to assume that vocabulary learning flows from reading rather than listening, which makes it important to show them how the spoken language is a suitable site for noticing useful chunks of language. Various terms have been used for this sort of noticing, including 'scavenging' (Sherman 1998), 'mining' (Samuda 2001), and 'foraging' (Schumann 2001). My preference is for 'quarrying', because of its natural association with chunks of material which are destined for use in physical construction, just as new second language chunks can be used in future linguistic constructions. The SAC video study notes below were written for international students attending a pre-sessional, English for Academic Purposes course at the University of Edinburgh. They highlight the academic content and language of the video materials available in the SAC, which are mostly science documentaries. The aim of the eight transcript tasks suggested in the notes is to familiarize the students with the idea of noticing and learning vocabulary from the spoken language through its written representation.

SAC—Notes on working with video transcripts
Below are eight language study activities you could do with a transcript.

1 Comparing transcript and soundtrack
Transcripts usually come with a note that they are adaptations from the soundtrack. Listen and read the transcript very carefully. Listen out for any differences between what the speaker says and what is on the page. Underline any changes and make a note of what the speaker actually said. Discuss with someone else possible reasons for the changes.

2 New language
Underline any expressions or words you haven't seen before. Can you work out their meaning? If not, ask or look them up.

3 Chains of reference
Choose one page of transcript and look for words/phrases that are linked in some way. Circle them and join them up. For example:

– alternative words for the same thing, for example, 'aim', 'objective', 'goal'
– textual links, for example, situation – problem – solution – evaluation
– different hypotheses to explain the same phenomenon
– time expressions showing the historical development of a concept.

4 Academic value
Choose two pages of transcript. Study them and highlight any expressions that you think are going to be useful to you in your future studies. Tell someone else why you've chosen them.

5 Background
Pick out a proper noun (person, place, organizational acronym, etc.). Look it up in an online encyclopedia and write a short glossary note, providing as much background as possible for another listener who is unfamiliar with the word in question. Add it to the SAC Video File.

6 As you said…
Look for examples in the transcript where one speaker *repeats* or *paraphrases* what the previous speaker has said. This is obviously most common in question/ answer linking in interviews, but you will also find it in discussion and conversations.

7 In others' words
Find examples of words whose meaning you have understood in this context but would have said differently yourself—for example, a speaker who says 'There's room for improvement' means something like 'It could have been done better'. Think how you would have said what the speaker in the video said.

8 For immediate use
Find an expression in the transcript that you think you will have a chance to use later today. (Try to use it before midnight!)

(adapted from IALS 1997)

Using comparators in self-access

My final suggestion for SAC listening is more speculative; it is something I have used in embryonic form (Lynch 2009b), but it has not yet been implemented on a large scale. What I have in mind is that the teachers working in a second language institution would gradually compile a database of digital recordings of native and non-native speakers performing the classroom tasks featured in their speaking courses. The recordings, which I have called 'comparators'—a comparator being 'a device for comparing something with a similar thing or with a standard measure' (*Longman Dictionary of the English Language* 1984)—would then be saved to the institution's intranet, to be accessed by individual learners working in the SAC. Transcripts of the recordings would also be saved to the intranet.

The learners could choose whether and when to listen to the comparator recording and to read the transcript. The comparators could be used at the

Pre-task stage, some time before the relevant speaking lesson. Once they have decided to use a comparator, they would choose either the native or the non-native recording. (For discussion of learners' attitudes to these alternatives, see Lynch 2009b.) Table 10.2 outlines what I have in mind for the use of comparators in a second language role-play task.

During the Task cycle (in the classroom) some activities would be obligatory, with the teacher monitoring performance and making notes. In Table 10.2 there is one obligatory task, marked with a cross, in which the learners would

PRE-TASK	**Self-access centre**		NS audio/video NS transcript NS audio/video NS transcript etc.
TASK CYCLE	**Classroom**	**X**	Private performance in parallel pairs Audio recording of parallel pairs Public performance by one pair Audio/video recording of 'public' pair etc.
POST-TASK (LANGUAGE STUDY)	**Classroom**		Teacher feedback on parallel pairs
			Proof-listening during 'public' replay • self feedback (from recorded pair) • peer feedback (from rest of class) • teacher feedback
			Speaking log during 'parallel' replay • teacher review of (response to) log
			Self-transcribing of 'parallel' replay • editing of transcript • reformulation by teacher • discussion of teacher's version
			Repetition of task with previous partner Repetition of task in new pairs
	or		etc.
	Self-access centre		NS audio/video NS transcript NNS audio/video NNS transcript Repetition of task with previous partner Repetition of task in new pairs etc.

Table 10.2 A framework for using comparators in a role-play task

work on a 'private' performance with a partner. The teacher would then select one pair to do a 'public' performance for the rest of the class. Before embarking on the task, the teacher would involve the learners in discussing whether they wanted to record themselves during their parallel pair work and whether the teacher should record the performance by the 'public' pair.

Decisions on Post-task (Language study) activities would be devolved to individual learners. They could opt for any of a number of listening-to-notice activities, such as self-transcribing, which would involve a combination of individual work, pair work, and discussion with the teacher (Lynch 2007). In addition, or instead, a learner might choose to repeat the task with a new partner, and then listen to their two recordings. At some stage they might decide to move to the SAC to listen to comparator materials there; again, they would have a choice of a native or non-native recording (if they had not listened to them at the Pre-task stage), or the version they did not listen to at the Pre-task stage, or possibly they might choose to read the transcript of the version they listened to before the class. In short, the comparator framework represents a menu of choices to be made by each individual learner, according to their perceptions of what will help them most, and in which order. In a broader sense, the use of comparators in self-access listening is intended to encourage learners' involvement in discussion (and decisions) about their individual learning preferences.

Summary

The objective of the learner-centred activities described in this chapter is to focus on the listener rather than the text, and to encourage the comparison and evaluation of individuals' interpretations of what a speaker meant, rather than to direct their attention solely to what the speaker actually said, as has tended to be the case in conventional comprehension questions. When it comes to self-access listening, we should be aiming to provide second language learners with an alternative to the sort of materials and tasks they will be using in the classroom, rather than simply to duplicate what is done in class with a teacher. The 'self-access' dimension of SAC listening materials need not be limited to listening for short-term comprehension; we should look for ways of helping learners to exploit listening materials as input for longer-term learning.

Suggestions for further reading

Littlewood, W. 1997. 'Self-access: Why do we want it and what can it do?' in P. Benson and P. Voller (eds.). *Autonomy and Independence in Language Learning*. London: Longman.

Morrison, B. 2008. 'The role of the self-access centre in the tertiary language learning process.' *System* 36/2: 123–40.

Nunan, D. 1997. 'Designing and adapting materials to encourage learner autonomy' in P. Benson and P. Voller (eds.). *Autonomy and Independence in Language Learning*. London: Longman.

Sheerin, S. 1989. *Self-Access*. Oxford: Oxford University Press. Still a valuable compendium of practical ideas.

Discussion and study questions

1 If there is a SAC where you teach, how do the students use it for listening? Do they listen to materials specified by their class teacher, or do they decide themselves which materials to listen to?

2 Some researchers have analysed how individual learners work with listening materials in self-access—how long they let a recording run before they replay parts of it, how often they listen to certain parts of a recording, whether they make notes, at what stage they refer to a transcript, and so on. Do you think this sort of observational research is relevant to designing SAC listening activities?

3 I have advocated classroom activities intended to bring out the differences between different listeners' interpretations, on the basis that such differences provide a natural platform for discussion. This is a popular activity with my students, who are adult learners of English. Do you think it would work with younger learners?

11 LISTENING BEYOND THE CLASSROOM

Introductory task

Some years ago I observed an intermediate-level English class in Edinburgh, in which the teacher was using a well-known listening comprehension text-book. As the lesson was about to end, the following exchange took place:

STUDENT   Why you don't give us real English?
TEACHER   What do you mean by 'real English'?
STUDENT   English like they speak it outside.

Before I tell you what the teacher's reply was, I would like you to imagine, first, that you are the learner. Why would you ask that particular question? What evidence might you have that the English you encounter in class is different from what is used outside the classroom?

Then imagine you are the teacher. Would you interpret the learner's question as a genuine question or a criticism? Is there some way you could turn it into an opportunity?

In fact, what the teacher said in response to the learner's question was 'because you wouldn't understand it if we did'. Do you think that was a reasonable reply to the learner's question?

Bringing the world into the classroom

Chapter 10 focused on ways of helping learners towards more independent listening and learning within an institutional setting—either in the conventional classroom or the self-access centre. Much of the literature on self-access learning is limited in two ways: firstly, discussion often focuses on issues of physical layout, reference systems, and technology, rather than on educational philosophy; and secondly, it seems to treat self-access as an end rather than a means. In his contribution to the authoritative collection *Autonomy and Independence in Language Learning* (Benson and Voller 1997), Andrew

Littlejohn criticized the second of these limitations: 'It is as if the notion of self-access work has no significance beyond the walls of the language teaching institution and in other areas of learners' lives' (Littlejohn 1997: 188–9).

One way of preparing learners for listening 'beyond the walls' is to bring the world into the classroom, by gathering recordings of authentic texts for learners to listen to, discuss, and analyse. Nearly two decades ago Elaine Tarone and George Yule, then working at the University of Minnesota, offered a comprehensive blueprint for a learner-centred second language programme based on 'a philosophy of local solutions to local problems' (Tarone and Yule 1989: 11). They developed an approach to second language teaching that was based on a conviction that what their students—mainly international graduates preparing for study at the university—needed was to find out 'how native speakers of a language go about accomplishing things in comparable situations' (Tarone and Yule 1989: 27) and then to use that as the basis for language study. They argued that the key was to involve the learners as data gatherers and discourse analysts. This was not a novel concept; in their book they acknowledge a local study in language course design by Kathryn Hanges (Hanges 1982), inspired by the work of the Brazilian educational philosopher Paulo Freire—and, specifically, the belief that 'learners themselves can, with guidance, provide valuable information about those situations in which they need to use the language' (Tarone and Yule 1989: 46). The basic procedure for their learner-centred course design can be summarized as follows:

1 Plan for interaction
The teacher helps the students to select the social situations and speech events which are relevant and problematic, and which they want to study in depth.

2 Interact
Learners go out into the world (for example, the university campus) and record interaction in those situations, involving either native speakers or themselves and native speakers.

3 Transcribe
The recordings are brought to class and everyone is involved in transcribing them.

4 Reflect
The learners as a group analyse what was being achieved through language use in the interaction. They address such issues as the roles of the participants, their relative status, the 'agenda' of each utterance, and the linguistic clues to attitude.

(based on Tarone and Yule 1989: 99–100)

The idea of using recordings gathered by second language learners as input to listening and analysis activities has now been adopted in a number of English-medium university settings. Learners have been guided to analyse content course tutorials in Scotland (Anderson and Lynch 1996), on-campus interviews in Australia (Clennell 1999), small-group discussions in New Zealand (Basturkmen 2002), and voluntary service placements in the USA (Hillyard, Reppen, and Vásquez 2007), for example. Interestingly, none of those studies referred directly to the work of Elaine Tarone and George Yule, but their book remains the most detailed practical discussion of what principled learner-centred teaching might involve. It is an excellent example of genuine 'applied linguistics'—linguistic theories applied to resolve a local problem—bringing the spoken language of the real world into the second language classroom, to allow its analysis by learners and teacher.

Moving beyond the classroom

As an alternative to bringing authentic language data into the classroom, one can look for ways 'to empower foreign language students to make effective use of the potential language-learning materials that exist around them'(Ryan 1997: 215). Although the availability of second language materials and interactions has tended to vary widely from place to place, the spread of digital technology is starting to erode the conventional distinction between 'foreign language' and 'second language' settings. 'The world has changed considerably in the past twenty-five years, one of the consequences being a vast proliferation of visible and audible samples of English, even in remote areas' (Field 2007: 36).

The potential availability of such practice materials raises a more general point about the relationship between the classroom and what happens outside it, which was recently made by David Crabbe of Victoria University in New Zealand. He argued that, although a great deal of principled ingenuity has gone into the design of effective and engaging classroom tasks, tasks are not an end in themselves. Teachers still need to develop ways of helping learners to turn their experience of tasks into something that they can apply *for themselves* beyond the classroom: 'language learning tasks are not a learning technology—they are a framework for learners' communicative performance and reflection on that performance' (Crabbe 2007: 117). David Crabbe proposed the term 'learning opportunity' to refer to a specific cognitive or metacognitive activity that a learner can engage in which is likely to lead to learning. I offer three examples of projects set up to encourage learners to venture outside the classroom into what I call 'the world out there' (WOT), in order to access and exploit real-life listening resources—to realize the sort of learning opportunities that David Crabbe may have had in mind. The projects come from three learning contexts— English as a second language, English as a foreign language, and Japanese as a second language.

WOT Project 1: English as a second language (Edinburgh, Scotland)

Since 1994 my colleague Kenneth Anderson and I have worked on several generations of materials designed to help learners to bridge the gap between the classroom and real life (Anderson and Lynch 1996, 2007). We resorted to three main sources in preparing our materials: firstly, the literature on second language acquisition and strategy training—in particular, Rubin and Thompson (1982); secondly, classroom methodology books, such as Harmer (1987), McCarthy (1991), and Nunan (1991); thirdly, and crucially, we elicited experience-based advice from international students on degree courses in Edinburgh. We wrote to around 100 graduate students, asking them to describe any language improvement techniques they had devised themselves and had found useful during their stay in Edinburgh. Their contribution was invaluable. Very few language teachers—ourselves included—have first-hand knowledge of what it is like to improve one's level in a second language while studying another (non-language) subject in the second-language setting.

These three sources—researchers, methodologists, and learners—provided a 'natural' structure for each unit: an introduction to key ideas from applied linguistic research; a description of practical resources that learners might exploit; and suggestions offered by past students, sharing their first-hand experience. This three-part structure also gave us the eventual title of our materials—*PROFILE - Principles, Resources, and Options for the Independent Learner of English*—which are designed for the lone learner without access to a teacher or a class. The extract below reproduces part of the Options section, which reports our students' recommendations for listening.

1 I noticed that I improved much more when I got a TV but I didn't take any conscious steps to practise listening.

2 In lectures they give us lots of notes, especially for the MSc classes. That made it easier and the subject was very familiar to me, so I could use my knowledge to work out what the lecturers were saying. I try to read the handouts again later, to fix the new information.

3 Listening to a tape and writing down exactly what you hear is very helpful. To listen very specifically and in detail means you have to pay attention to sounds which you have some problems with yourself. Seeing what the gaps are in your dictation tells you what your listening problems are.

4 I listen to the news on television or radio and then try to discuss the topics with friends. This is very useful for me to know whether the news that I have heard is correct and does not give different perspectives than my understanding.

5 I improve listening by meeting a lot of friends and talking to them on any topic. The best way is to make them give explanations when I don't

understand something and then to tell them what I have understood from those explanations.

6 I spend quite a lot of time listening to the radio, such as the news on Radio 4, which is good practice. Especially when some of the news is repeated, that helps me to confirm what I have heard.

7 Watching an interesting movie or TV programme such as the Cosby Show will attract my attention to follow the story and hence practise my English by listening.

8 I think it's good practice to listen to other foreign speakers talking about your field. You have to get used to their accents, in the same way as you have to get used to British people's different accents. In fact, there are bigger differences between British accents than between foreigners, I think. So it's all good practice and helps to find out more about the subject.

(Anderson and Lynch 1996: 26)

The Listening unit illustrates two principal aims of the *PROFILE* project. Firstly, we wanted to encourage newly arrived students to take a positive approach to managing their problems with English. Secondly, we wanted to make them aware that the best place to encounter realistic learning materials is their daily WOT contact with English in their lives as university students, rather than in the second language classroom. (For further details of *PROFILE*, see Lynch 2001.)

WOT Project 2: English as a foreign language (Osaka, Japan)

My EFL example is a project devised by Stephen Ryan at Osaka Institute of Technology (Ryan 1997). His teaching context was, on the face of it, rather unpromising: a compulsory general English course for final-year engineering students with relatively low motivation, since any real need for English was likely to be some years in the future, when they might be sent abroad by their companies and would have to use English for professional and social purposes. Stephen Ryan's aim was to show the students how they might continue to improve their English independently by making use of materials in the world around them. The topics covered in the Osaka project were very much the same as those in *PROFILE*, though in a different sequence: to raise the students' awareness of the resources available, to practise techniques for exploiting them, and to introduce parts of second language acquisition theory underlying those techniques. Each unit of the course focused on a different kind of resource, such as print media, videos, and native speakers.

As far as listening comprehension was concerned, Stephen Ryan pointed out to his students that various features of the Japanese media environment favoured learners of English who wanted to improve their listening skills independently: foreign films shown on television used a multiplex system that allowed viewers to select either the English or the Japanese soundtrack; and films shown in cinemas and rented out from video shops preserved the original English soundtrack with Japanese subtitles. The availability of Japanese-language soundtrack or subtitles allowed the learners to check their own comprehension of what they had watched. This helped resolve a perennial problem of listening for the independent learner, namely, 'to ensure that [the techniques] do not require the cooperation of somebody more fluent in English than the learner' (Ryan 1997: 220). Stephen Ryan helped the students to understand WOT audio and video news materials by using parallel texts, such as Japanese press reports on the news story they had watched in English.

One difference between this project and *PROFILE* lies in their overall philosophies of learner education. For Stephen Ryan's engineering students, the final part of the course involved an evaluation of alternative listening techniques, presented by the teacher, in the light of ideas from second language acquisition theory: 'a careful explanation of *why a particular technique is good (or bad)* can be helpful in bringing each student towards autonomy' (Ryan 1997: 223, my italics). That seems to imply that language teachers know what the most effective techniques for language learning are and can 'reveal' them to learners. This contrasts with our approach in *PROFILE*, which is to pass on, in the Options section of each unit, *all* the options recommended by our international students and to offer them as techniques that our readers should try out for themselves, without being filtered through the value judgements of a teacher.

WOT Project 3: Japanese as a second language (Tokushima, Japan)

Both the projects I have discussed so far began in the 1990s, before the dramatic expansion of the Internet. My third example is a project which adopted a more technological approach to helping learners of Japanese take their listening beyond the classroom: the project has the acronym *LOCH* (Language-learning Outside the Classroom with Handhelds). It was the result of collaboration between six researchers in informatics and two teachers of Japanese from the International Students Center at Tokushima University (Paredes, Ogata, Saito, Yin, Yano, Oishi, and Ueda 2005). In *LOCH* the teachers set the students a series of listening and speaking tasks, which they have to carry out in the local area. To enable them to complete the tasks, each learner is given a Toshiba PDA (Personal Digital Assistant) with GPS (Global Positioning System) and PHS (Personal Handy System). That combination of devices gives them access to their own language learning data, video, and audio files. They can also access Internet information and record their interactions with native speakers, and—via the PHS—call each other and the teacher when they are moving around the city working on a learning task. The teacher is able to track each learner's position via GPS. Here are two examples of the sort of task that *LOCH* learners have to carry out:

> Go to the touristic information stand in Tokushima [railway] station, and enquire about the places you can visit in just one day and the price. Record the answer of the stand attendant and send it back. (Paredes *et al.* 2005: 3)

> Go to the Awaodori Kaikan, and enquire about price and schedule of the rope way. Bring back the schedule and send the recording of the characteristic music of the Awaodori, continuously playing inside the building, and a picture of the souvenirs displayed in the shop. (Paredes *et al.* 2005: 3–4)

The overall tone of the research team's report was extremely upbeat: 'wireless mobile learning devices offer stunning technical capabilities for the development of new systems, because of their portability and low cost' (Paredes *et al.* 2005: 1). As I suggested at the beginning of this book, technology has tended to run ahead of pedagogic principles and applications. In Chapter 10, I referred to the dangers of technology-*driven* teaching, and *LOCH* strikes me as a very clear example of what can go wrong—on many different levels— when what is technically feasible is assumed to be pedagogically appropriate. The researchers make strong claims for the success of the project:

> The teachers were more reachable and the knowledge became more available due to the IP phone … the students could easily reach the teacher when having troubles and the teachers could immediately redirect them when they were not achieving the expected results. (Paredes *et al.* 2005: 4–5)

However, they do not discuss the nature of the knowledge that 'became available', or what they actually mean by the teacher 'redirecting' the learners, and they seem unaware of the limitations of getting learners to work on tasks with 'expected'—in other words, entirely predictable—results, in terms of information collected.

The *LOCH* learners are given a very specific set of tasks by a teacher who is able, literally, to monitor their progress through those tasks by using GPS. They video- and audio-record the answers they get from the people to whom they are instructed to speak, and they send those answers back to the teacher. Potentially, they could make effective use of the data for further classroom work, but in fact no such activities are described in the paper. Furthermore, while the element of 'control' in the Computer column of Table 1.1 was control by the learner of the learning material, in the *LOCH* project control is exerted by the teacher or task designer over the actions of the learners. It would be hard to imagine a greater difference in learner initiative and responsibility than that between the box-ticking type of information task set in *LOCH* and the language data-gathering and analysis of Elaine Tarone and George Yule's approach of two decades earlier.

Some listening resources for the independent learner

Narrow listening

This is a technique devised by Stephen Krashen in his independent learning of Spanish (Krashen 1996). He recommends it for second language acquirers—that is, people who are not attending formal language classes—who find that normal-speed conversation is beyond their current level. Narrow listening involves finding a native speaker with a few minutes to spare, and who is willing to be recorded. The learner chooses a topic which they are interested in, and which they know the native speaker will know something about, and asks them to talk about it for two or three minutes. The recording can then be played back as many times as the learner wants to hear it; Stephen Krashen says he listens to his Spanish recordings while driving and finds that each time he listens he understands a bit more. The unique advantage of narrow listening is that the recordings are dedicated, in the sense that the speaker is talking to and for the individual learner, and on subjects that the learner has chosen. A further advantage is that the listener will have had access to the original visual context, which is likely to assist their understanding in the later listenings.

B.C. Dupuy reported on the use of narrow listening within a formal teacher-led programme in French as a second language at Louisiana State University (Dupuy 1999). An experiment involving 255 students at different French proficiency levels found significant improvement in learners' self-reported listening comprehension (and to a lesser extent in their fluency and vocabulary). It also showed, not surprisingly, that the benefits were greater for learners at the two lowest proficiency levels. Although these are positive findings, it seems to me that the greater value of narrow listening lies in its use by the independent learner, rather than in its classroom or self-access use.

Listening websites

Interestingly, so far none of our *PROFILE* informants in Edinburgh has mentioned using any of the dedicated second language listening websites now set up for English learners. Perhaps they were unaware of them, or had tried some sites but found them unsuitable for their particular listening needs. Perhaps students who are already functioning in a second language environment feel it would be a backward step to use materials meant for learners, as opposed to users, of the language? However, for the many learners of English in foreign language settings, there are a number of excellent sites now available and I offer the list below as a starting point.

ABC radio http://www.abc.net.au/radio

Andy Gillett's academic English learning website http://www.uefap.com/links/linkfram.htm

BBC World Service http://www.bbc.co.uk/worldservice

British Library Education Service http://www.bl.uk/learning (Mainly reading material, but with some links to audio and video archive material.)

CBS radio http://www.cbsradio.com

CNN http://cnn.com

English Listening Lounge http://www.englishlistening.com

ESL Café http://www.eslcafe.com

E-views: Accents in English http://www.eviews.net (Very good, but currently being redesigned. Not a free service.)

International Lyrics Playground http://www.lyricsplayground.com (For songs.)

Randall's ESL Cyber Listening Lab http://www.esl-lab.com

Voice of America http://www.voanews.com/english/about

It is in the nature of the Internet that websites come and go, so for an up-to-date list of the listening websites I recommend, you are welcome to visit http://www.ials.ed.ac.uk/TonyLynchhomepage.htm.

Extensive listening

Extensive reading is a well-established part of many second language programmes, usually involving a combination of classroom reading of simple reader stories and homework or spare time reading. The term 'extensive listening' has been coined to describe the oral equivalent of extensive reading. (Of course, storytelling is oral in origin, but the use of second language stories still tends to be associated with the written word.) There is now growing interest in using story listening, especially for lower-level and/or younger second language learners. A recent study in Spain found that primary school pupils who listened individually (through headphones) to digital English stories on the Web made greater improvements in their listening comprehension than others who listened to conventional material in textbook-based classes (Ramírez and Alonso 2007). The researchers ascribed this improvement to greater levels of concentration and focused attention, and possibly to the additional motivation in using digital materials where the listener 'participates' by deciding when to move on to the next part of the story.

It seems reasonable to argue that adult learners, too, would benefit from extensive listening, but very little research has been done to demonstrate its benefits. One of the leading advocates of this approach is Rob Waring, an English teacher working at Notre Dame University in Japan; the materials he recommends are mainly the read-aloud audio-recordings that accompany some published simple reader books, rather than spoken-language versions of simple stories. Some years ago he asked, 'Why has our field completely ignored the need for graded fluency listening input that is for pleasure, aimed at building listening recognition speed and automaticity?' (Waring 2006) and that question has so far not received an adequate answer. Cambridge University Press recently announced a plan to offer graded listening materials in MP3 format (Cambridge University Press 2007) but that appears still to be in the pipeline.

Other people

We should not allow the apparently exciting prospects for one-way listening based on digital media to lead us to neglect the potential learning opportunities of two-way listening with our fellow human beings—either face-to-face, which is how I have learnt my languages, or at a distance, using interactive forms of electronic technology, such as webcams and webcall software such as Skype. 'Off-the-shelf technology is not ready for interactive oral-aural instruction' (Robin 2007: 109); some authors have suggested that learners should use 'chatterbots'—artificial intelligence programs that are intended to simulate interaction with a human—but they seem to me to be still too limited for any use other than amusement. I recently tried interacting with Jabberwacky, supposedly one of the more advanced chatterbots, and the 'conversation' went like this:

JABBERWACKY	How are you?
TONY	I'm a little down.
JABBERWACKY	How old are you?
TONY	What's it to you?
JABBERWACKY	I'm just curious.
TONY	Well, I'm 59.
JABBERWACKY	You are old.
TONY	I always say you're as old as you feel.
JABBERWACKY	How old are you?
	etc.

Although I *have* had similar conversations with people, I usually try to avoid talking to them a second time.

Interacting with real people is not only more stimulating, but it appears to bring tangible benefits for listening. In a survey conducted among the international student population at the University of Edinburgh, I found that the amount of progress they reported in understanding spoken English during their first six months in Britain correlated positively with the number of minutes they estimated they spent each week in conversation (listening/speaking) with other users of English—not necessarily native speakers—but not with the time spent on one-way listening (Lynch 2006). Below are the

comments of students who reported the most progress and also made the greatest improvement in scores on a one-way listening test:

Cuban student

When I arrived here I felt quite rejected because my English was not very clear as I would like it to be. But that's wrong, I changed my mind immediately. The best way to improve your English is to speak freely with people even if your English is not very good. People here are sensitive when they realize you are not a native. They help you. They don't correct you but they pay attention and they make an effort to understand you, and they answer your questions in the best way they can. The other thing is to use the facilities—the Institute, online facilities—and try to avoid speaking your language.

Chinese student

The more you listen, the better you understand. It's very good to listen to different accents here, like Australian English. If you come here, you can make friends with different nations. That's very important. I have Italian and Spanish friends and their English is always simple and easy to understand.

As I have stressed in this book, one-way listening and two-way listening require different skills; by negotiating meaning in conversation when problems arise, learners may be able to access new language, or retrieve 'submerged' language, which is then activated to feed in to their success in understanding it on a later occasion. I believe that, for the moment, conversation with other people is the only effective 'site' for learners to learn to negotiate, and to negotiate to learn.

Learning and teaching listening in the future?

If we think back to the four Listeners in Chapter 1—the radio fan, the TV viewer, the iPod owner, and the laptop user—one thing they had in common is that none of them talked about using listening materials intended for language teaching. The main difference between language learning today and language learning when I started German and French at school in the 1960s is learners' easier access to non-pedagogic texts—what Richard Robin of George Washington University has called 'the "raw" electronic world' (Robin

2007: 113), in contrast to second language materials pre-packaged for language learning. It is difficult to predict precisely how technology will change in the next generation, but one thing is certain: tomorrow's learners will have a higher level of media literacy—competence to 'decode, analyze, evaluate, and produce both print and electronic media' (Aufderheide 1997: 79)—than is common today.

The possible effects of children's earlier acquisition of the skills of media use and the knowledge of media conventions were recently discussed by Paul Gruba of the University of Melbourne, who offered teachers an insight into the future of language teaching. He drew in particular on the work of media literacy specialist Margaret Mackey of the University of Alberta, who has argued that 'play' should replace 'read' as the generic verb to describe what people do when they process a text (Mackey 2002). Her notion of playing with a text (print or electronic) embraces various aspects of user involvement: imagining, performing, engaging with the rules of the game, strategizing, orchestrating, interpreting, exploring, and reflecting (Gruba 2006: 79). Margaret Mackey's ideas of textual play were developed to apply to media literacy in the first language, but Paul Gruba has teased out their potential implications for incorporating media literacy into second language instruction:

> An ideal lesson would draw student attention to verbal and visual elements that have a particularly significant cultural meaning in context . . . Extended discussion would then draw out analysis and evaluation of the social, historical, and political implications of key elements . . . By introducing media literacy concepts throughout our syllabus we can encourage our students to play with video texts and undertake a journey of discovery. (Gruba 2006: 87)

This opens up intriguing possibilities, but one thing that seems to be missing from this vision of future video-based listening instruction is *language*; the 'ideal lesson' seems to assume second language learners at an advanced level of proficiency. For those of us working with lower-level students, the trick will still be to devise techniques for helping learners to 'play with' texts in order to bring out both their meaning(s)—the focus of Paul Gruba's study—and also the specific language forms in which meaning was expressed. These techniques should, if possible, be ones that language learners can transfer to independent work with audio and video materials beyond the classroom, to realize the 'learning opportunities' that David Crabbe described.

Michael Rost's preferred term for the techniques that teachers use to teach listening is 'interventions'. In a recent article (Rost 2007) he described the different interventions he has found appropriate in the three elements of listening that we considered in Part Two of this book—Recognition, Interpretation, and Participation—and suggested ways of using new technology to manage those interventions. From his experience of teaching learners of English, in both second and foreign language settings and at a wide range of levels, he concluded:

> A major part of our job as teachers is to *know our students*—to know which aspects of listening our students tend to avoid, to know which goals are hardest for them to achieve, in short, to know which specific interventions will actually *help* them.(Rost 2007: 4)

That seems to me to be a suitably challenging and inspiring note on which to end this book. Knowing our students, knowing how listening works, and knowing what materials and activities help individuals listen more effectively, have always been at the core of second language listening instruction. What is new today is the sheer variety of listening resources that our students can access. The challenge for teachers is to find ways of helping learners to access them directly, when and where it suits them, beyond the classroom.

Suggestions for further reading

Gruba, P. 2006. 'Playing the videotext: A media literacy perspective on video-mediated L2 listening.' *Language Learning and Technology* 10/2: 77–92.

Lynch, T. 2001. 'Promoting EAP learner autonomy in a second language university context' in J. Flowerdew and M. Peacock (eds.). *Research Perspectives on English for Academic Purposes*. Cambridge: Cambridge University Press. An account of the development of the *PROFILE* project at Edinburgh.

Rost, M. 2007. 'Commentary: *I'm only trying to help*: A role for interventions in teaching listening.' *Language Learning and Technology* 11/1: 102–8.

Discussion and study questions

1 Discuss with your teaching colleagues how they respond to the suggestions in this chapter that we should encourage second language learners to gain additional listening practice and experience outside the institutional setting. Do they raise any objections? If so, are they concerned about expense, logistics, or wider ethical issues?

2 Assuming you encounter no serious objections (Question 1), carry out a survey among your colleagues asking whether they have recommended listening websites to their students. Then do a similar survey of your second language students, asking them which listening sites they use or have used. Compare your findings from the two surveys. Is there some way of making the knowledge of the two groups (learners and teachers) available to all the learners in your institution?

3 It is possible that by the time you read this book, we will be able to access free or cheap speech recognition software that will allow second language speakers to talk directly to chatterbots (also called 'chat bots', 'voice bots', and 'chatterboxes'). If so, ask your students to visit Jabberwacky at http://www.jabberwacky.com/ and have a conversation. If suitable voice recognition software is not available, the students can key in their turns in the dialogue. When they have finished, get them to copy and paste the on-screen text. They (and you) can then discuss how natural they felt the 'conversation' was.

GLOSSARY

The definitions here reflect the terms as I have used them in this book. Other writers may use them in different ways.

Adjustment (modification): A change made by a speaker, either to input or interaction, in order to help the listener understand.

Bottom-up processing: Step-by-step decoding of a text, beginning with the sounds and gradually building up larger units of meaning. Contrasted with **top-down**.

Cognitive strategies: Strategies used by a listener to focus on what is being said, such as listening out for stressed syllables and guessing from context.

Communication strategies: An umbrella term for techniques used to cope with current difficulties in understanding or producing the second language.

Communication Theory (or Mathematical Theory of Communication): A statistical view of communication in which the importance of the elements of a message was measured in terms of their predictability in the sequence of sounds.

Comprehensible input: A second language message which may include words and structures above the listener's current proficiency level, but which can be understood on the basis of context, visual clues, and relevant background knowledge.

Connectionism: The theory that knowledge and learning rely on the gradual strengthening of a network of associated memories.

Constructed-response item: A question that requires the listener to create their own answer, such as by writing words into a gap. Used in contrast to **selected-response item**.

Content schemata: A person's knowledge of the topic they are currently listening to.

Conversational adjustment (interaction adjustment): A change made by a speaker to the pattern of interaction, such as checking the listener has understood, to prevent or repair non-comprehension.

Co-text: The other parts of a text preceding and following the item currently being processed.

Dictogloss: An activity in which learners hear a text once or twice at natural speed and then try to reconstruct it from their notes.

Expectancy grammar: The internal system of knowledge and experience of the second language that allows the listener to process utterances and assign meanings to them.

Foreigner talk: Speech modified to be accessible to a second language listener.

Formal schemata: A listener's knowledge of typical text-types or genres.

Free talk: A listening and speaking activity in which each learner nominates a topic or question for discussion in groups.

Genre: A type of text recognizable by its form and function—for example, a joke or a prayer.

Global query: Non-specific clarification request from a listener, such as 'Pardon?' or 'I don't understand'. Used in contrast to **local queries**.

Inference: A listener's interpretation of something which is not stated explicitly but which can be understood from the context.

Information processing: A view of communication and learning that regards the human brain as a computer with a comparatively limited processing capacity, so that when we pay particular attention to one aspect of a spoken message, we have to divert attention from other aspects.

Interlocutor: A participant in a conversation.

Lexical selection: The process by which the listener identifies a word in the stream of speech.

Linguistic adjustment (input adjustment): A modification made to the form of what a speaker says, such as grammatical tense or choice of words, to help a listener understand.

Local query: Clarification request from a listener that locates the source of their current comprehension problem, such as 'How many times did you say she asked?' or 'What was the word before "cellars"?'

Mental model: The listener's current internal picture of the message a speaker is trying to convey.

Metacognitive strategies: Listening strategies that involve planning, monitoring, and evaluating comprehension.

Modification: The process of simplifying a text, or a change made in that process, especially in the case of spoken communication.

Negotiation of meaning: The mutual process by which participants try to ensure that they understand, and are understood by, each other, by means of comprehension checks, clarification requests, and so on.

Orchestration: Effective coordination of different listening strategies or skills.

Pacing: The tempo at which stressed syllables are spoken, expressed as a figure per minute.

Parallel distributed processing: Simultaneous use of information from different sources (sounds, visual context, background knowledge, etc.) to understand a message.

Parsing: Analysis of the grammatical structure of an utterance.

Personal-response item: A form of assessment that focuses on and encourages the listener's subjective reaction to a text, rather than on its objective content.

Phonological decoding: The process by which a listener converts sounds into words.

Post-modification: Adjustment made to a recording to make it easier for learners to understand, for example, by editing, or slowing it down.

Pre-modification: Planned or scripted adjustments to a spoken text, in the interest of simplification.

Prosody: The characteristic combination of stress, rhythm, and intonation in a language.

Reformulation: Rephrasing something to make it more accessible to the listener.

Schema (plural **schemata**)**:** A mental structure comprising knowledge, memory, and experience, which allows listeners to incorporate what they hear into what they know.

Selected-response item: A test item, such as true/false or multiple choice, where the listener has to choose one of the answers offered.

Social Constructivism: Theory that human beings construct knowledge mainly from their interactions with others.

Socioaffective strategies: A range of strategies that involve encouraging oneself to be positive, or interacting with other people, when comprehension problems arise.

Sociocultural Theory: The theory that learning occurs through dialogue: knowledge is first constructed in face-to-face interaction, for example between parent and child, and then internalized by the individual. Associated with Lev Vygotsky.

Spacing: The proportion of stressed words in the total number of words a speaker produces, expressed as a ratio such as 1 to 4.

Speech rate: The average number of words or syllables that a speaker utters per minute.

Top-down processing: The listener's use of higher-level information, such as expectations and topic knowledge, to construct an interpretation of an incoming message.

BIBLIOGRAPHY

Aida, Y. 1994. 'Examination of Horwitz, Horwitz, and Cope's construct of foreign language anxiety: The case of students of Japanese.' *Modern Language Journal* 78/2: 155–68.

Anderson, A. and **T. Lynch.** 1988. *Listening.* Oxford: Oxford University Press.

Anderson, J. 1985. *Cognitive Psychology and its Implications.* New York, NY: Freeman.

Anderson, K. and **T. Lynch.** 1996. *PROFILE: Principles, Resources and Options for the Independent Learner of English.* Edinburgh: Institute for Applied Language Studies.

Anderson, K. and **T. Lynch.** 2007. *PROFILE: Principles, Resources and Options for the Independent Learner of English.* 2nd edition. Edinburgh: Institute for Applied Language Studies.

Anderson-Hsieh, J. and **K. Koehler.** 1988. 'The effect of foreign accent and speaking rate on native speaker comprehension.' *Language Learning* 38/4: 561–613.

Arnold, J. 2000. 'Seeing through listening comprehension exam anxiety'. *TESOL Quarterly* 34/4: 777–86.

Aufderheide, P. 1997. 'Media literacy: From a report of the National Leadership Conference on Media Literacy' in R. Kubey (ed.). *Media Literacy in the Information Age.* New Brunswick, NJ: Transaction.

Axbey, S. 1989. 'Standard exercises in self-access learning.' Presentation at British Council course on Self-Access Learning, Cambridge, May 1989.

Ayano, S. and **D. Hardison.** 2005. 'The role of gestures and facial cues in second language listening comprehension.' *Language Learning* 55/4: 661–99.

Bacon, S. 1992. 'The relationship between gender, comprehension, processing strategies, and cognitive and affective response in foreign language listening.' *Modern Language Journal* 76/2: 160–76.

Bahns, J. 1995. 'Retrospective review article: There's more to listening than meets the ear.' *System* 23/4: 531–47.

Bartlett, C. 1932. *Remembering*. Cambridge: Cambridge University Press.

Basturkmen, H. 2002. 'Learner observation of, and reflection on, spoken discourse: An approach for teaching academic speaking.' *TESOL Journal* 11/2: 26–30.

Bejarano, Y., T. Levine, E. Olshtain, and **J. Steiner.** 1997. 'The skilled use of interaction strategies: Creating a framework for improved small-group communicative interaction in the language classroom.' *System* 25/2: 203–14.

Bell, A. 1984. 'Language style as audience design.' *Language in Society* 13/2: 145–204.

Benson, P. and **P. Voller** (eds.). 1997. *Autonomy and Independence in Language Learning*. London: Longman.

Berquist, B. 1994. 'Memory models applied to L2 comprehension: A search for common ground' in G. Taillefer and A. Pugh (eds.). *Reading in the University: First, Second and Foreign Languages*. Toulouse: Presses de l'Université des Sciences Sociales de Toulouse.

Bilbow, G. 1989. 'Towards an understanding of overseas students' difficulties in lectures: A phenomenographic approach.' *Journal of Further and Higher Education* 13/2: 85–99.

Blundell L. and **J. Stokes.** 1981. *Task Listening—Teacher's Book*. Cambridge: Cambridge University Press.

Bremer, K., C. Roberts, M. Vasseur, M. Simonot, and **P. Broeder.** 1996. *Achieving Understanding: Discourse in International Encounters*. London: Longman.

Brett, P. 1995. 'Multimedia for listening comprehension: The design of a multimedia-based resource for developing listening skills.' *System* 23/1: 77–85.

Brindley, G. 1998. 'Assessing listening abilities.' *Annual Review of Applied Linguistics* 18: 171–91.

Brown, G. 1977. *Listening to Spoken English*. Harlow: Longman.

Brown, G. 1990. *Listening to Spoken English*. 2nd edition. Harlow: Longman.

Brown, G. 1995. *Speakers, Listeners and Communication*. Cambridge: Cambridge University Press.

Brown, G. 2008. 'Selective listening.' *System* 36/1: 10–21.

Brown, G., A. Anderson, R. Shillcock, and **G. Yule.** 1984. *Teaching Talk.* Cambridge: Cambridge University Press.

Brown, G., K. Malmkjaer, A. Pollitt, and **J. Williams** (eds.). 1994. *Language and Understanding.* Oxford: Oxford University Press.

Brown, G. and **G. Yule.** 1983a. *Teaching the Spoken Language.* Cambridge: Cambridge University Press.

Brown, G. and **G. Yule.** 1983b. *Discourse Analysis.* Cambridge: Cambridge University Press.

Brown, J. and **T. Hudson.** 1998. 'The alternatives in language assessment.' *TESOL Quarterly* 32/4: 653–75.

Buck, G. 1990. 'The testing of second language listening comprehension.' PhD thesis, Lancaster University.

Buck, G. 2001. *Assessing Listening.* Cambridge: Cambridge University Press.

Buck, G. and **K. Tatsuoka.** 1998. 'Application of the rule-space procedure to language testing: Examining attributes of a free response listening test.' *Language Testing* 15/2: 119–57.

Bygate, M. 1998. 'Theoretical perspectives on speaking.' *Annual Review of Applied Linguistics* 18: 20–42.

Cambridge University Press. 2007. *Cambridge Connection: Keeping Teachers Connected.* Japan edition #03.

Carrell, P. 1984. 'Evidence of a formal schema in second language comprehension.' *Language Learning* 18/3: 441–69.

Cauldwell, R. 1996. 'Direct encounters with fast speech on CD-audio to teach listening.' *System* 24/4: 521–28.

Chamot, A. 1995. 'Learning strategies and listening comprehension' in D. Mendelsohn and J. Rubin (eds.). *A Guide for the Teaching of Second Language Listening.* San Diego, CA: Dominie Press.

Chiang, C. and **P. Dunkel.** 1992. 'The effect of speech modification, prior knowledge, and listening proficiency on EFL lecture learning.' *TESOL Quarterly* 26/2: 345–74.

Clarke, M. 1979. 'Reading in Spanish and English: Evidence from adult ESL students.' *Language Learning* 29/1: 121–47.

Clennell, C. 1999. 'Promoting pragmatic awareness and spoken discourse skills with EAP classes.' *ELT Journal* 53/2: 83–93.

Conrad, L. 1985. 'Semantic versus syntactic cues in listening comprehension.' *Studies in Second Language Acquisition* 7/1: 59–72.

Cook, V. 1973. 'The comparison of language development in native children and foreign adults.' *International Review of Applied Linguistics* XI/1: 13–28.

Coupland, N. and **H. Bishop.** 2007. 'Ideological values for British accents.' *Journal of Sociolinguistics* 11/1: 74–93.

Crabbe, D. 2007. 'Learning opportunities: Adding value to tasks.' *ELT Journal* 61/2: 118–25.

Crystal, D. and **D. Davy.** 1975. *Advanced Conversational English.* Harlow: Longman.

Cutler, A. 1997. 'How can listeners find the right words?' Paper presented at IATEFL Research Group conference: Research meets practice—listening skills. Cambridge, England, March 1997.

Cutler, A. 2000. 'Listening to a second language through the ears of a first.' *Interpreting* 5/1: 1–23.

Cutler, A., D. Dahan, and **W. van Donselaar.** 1997. 'Prosody in the comprehension of spoken language: Literature review.' *Language and Speech* 40/2: 141–202.

Cutting, J. 2000. *Analysing the Language of Discourse Communities.* Oxford: Elsevier Science.

Dam Jensen, E. 1996. 'Enhancing oral input by means of interactive video.' Proceedings of the Computer Assisted Learning and Instruction Consortium (CALICO) Annual Symposium.

De Filippis, D. 1980. 'A study of the listening strategies used by skillful and unskillful college French students in aural comprehension tasks.' PhD dissertation, University of Pittsburgh.

Delabatie, B. and **D. Bradley.** 1995. 'Resolving word boundaries in spoken French: Native and non-native strategies.' *Applied Psycholinguistics* 16/1: 59–81.

Deulofeu, J. and **M. Taranger.** 1984. 'Relation entre le linguistique et le culturel—microscopie de quelques malentendus et incompréhensions' in C. Noyau and R. Porquier (eds.). *Communiquer dans la Langue de l'Autre.* Paris: Presses Universitaires de Vincennes.

Dickinson, L. and **R. Mackin.** 1969. *Varieties of Spoken English.* Oxford: Oxford University Press.

Dupoux, E., C. Pallier, N. Sebastian, and **J. Mehler.** 1997. 'A destressing 'deafness' in French?' *Journal of Memory and Language* 36: 406–21.

Dupuy, B. C. 1999. 'Narrow listening: An alternative way to develop and enhance listening comprehension in students of French as a foreign language.' *System* 27/3: 351–61.

Faerch, C. and **G. Kasper.** 1983. 'Plans and strategies in foreign language communication' in C. Faerch and G. Kasper (eds.). *Strategies in Interlanguage Communication*. Harlow: Longman.

Field, J. 1997. 'Monitoring for breakdown of understanding' in J. Field, A. Graham, E. Griffiths, and K. Head (eds.). *Teachers Develop Teachers Research: 2*. Whitstable, England: IATEFL.

Field, J. 1998. 'Skills and strategies: Towards a new methodology for listening.' *ELT Journal* 52/2: 110–18.

Field, J. 2000. 'Not waving but drowning: A reply to Tony Ridgway.' *ELT Journal* 54/2: 186–95.

Field, J. 2004. 'An insight into listeners' problems: Too much bottom-up or too much top-down?' *System* 32/3: 363–77.

Field, J. 2007. 'Looking outwards, not inwards.' *ELT Journal* 61/1: 30–8.

Field, J. 2008. 'Revising segmentation hypotheses in first and second language listening.' *System* 36/1: 35–51.

Flavell, J. 1976. 'Metacognitive aspects of problem solving' in L. B. Resnick (ed.). *The Nature of Intelligence*. Hillsdale, NJ: Lawrence Erlbaum.

Flowerdew, J. and **L. Miller.** 2005. *Second Language Listening*. Cambridge: Cambridge University Press.

Freedle, R. and **I. Kostin.** 1999. 'Does the text matter in a multiple-choice test of comprehension? The case for the construct validity of TOEFL's minitalks.' *Language Testing* 16/1: 2–32.

Fujita, J. 1984. 'A preliminary inquiry into the successful and unsuccessful strategies of beginning college Japanese students.' PhD dissertation, Ohio State University.

Gardner, R. 1998. 'Between speaking and listening: The vocalization of understanding.' *Applied Linguistics* 19/2: 204–24.

Garrett, N. 1991. 'Technology in the service of language teaching: Trends and issues.' *Modern Language Journal* 75/1: 74–101.

Garza, T. 1991. 'Evaluating the use of captioned video materials in advanced foreign language learning.' *Foreign Language Annals* 24/3: 239–58.

Gass, S. and **E. Varonis.** 1984. 'The effect of familiarity on the comprehensibility of non-native speech.' *Language Learning* 34/1: 65–89.

Goh, C. 1997. 'Metacognitive awareness and second language listeners.' *ELT Journal* 51/4: 361–69.

Goh, C. 2000. 'A cognitive perspective on language learners' listening comprehension problems.' *System* 28/1: 55–75.

Goh, C. 2002. 'Exploring listening comprehension tactics and their interaction patterns.' *System* 30/2: 185–206.

Goh, C. and **Y. Taib.** 2006. 'Metacognitive instruction in listening for young learners.' *ELT Journal* 60/3: 222–32.

Graham, S. 2006. 'Listening comprehension: The learners' perspective.' *System* 34/2: 165–82.

Graham, S., D. Santos, and **R. Vanderplank.** 2008. 'Listening comprehension and strategy use: A longitudinal exploration.' *System* 36/1: 52–68.

Griffiths, R. 1990. 'Speech rate and NNS comprehension: A preliminary study in time-benefit analysis.' *Language Learning* 40/3: 311–36.

Gruba, P. 2006. 'Playing the videotext: A media literacy perspective on video-mediated L2 listening.' *Language Learning and Technology* 10/2: 77–92.

Guichon, N. and **S. McLornan.** 2008. 'The effects of multimodality on L2 learners: Implications for CALL resource design.' *System* 36/1: 85–93.

Hanges, K. 1982. 'Course design for a composition/research skills class for international graduate students.' MA qualifying paper, ESL Program, University of Minnesota.

Harder, P. 1980. 'Discourse as self-expression: On the reduced personality of the second-language learner.' *Applied Linguistics* 1/3: 262–70.

Harmer, J. 1987. *Teaching and Learning Grammar*. Harlow: Longman.

Harmer, J. 2001. *The Practice of English Language Teaching* (3rd edition). London: Longman.

Harris, T. 2003. 'Listening with your eyes: The importance of speech-related gestures in the language classroom.' *Foreign Language Annals* 36/2: 180–7.

Hasan, A. 2000. 'Learners' perceptions of listening comprehension problems.' *Language, Culture and Curriculum* 13/2: 137–53.

Hatch, E. 1978. 'Discourse analysis in second language acquisition' in E. Hatch (ed.). *Second Language Acquisition*. Rowley, MA: Newbury House.

Hatch, E. 1992. *Discourse and Language Education*. Cambridge: Cambridge University Press.

Hawkins, B. 1985. 'Is an "appropriate response" always so appropriate?' in S. Gass and C. Madden (eds.). *Input in Second Language Acquisition.* Rowley, MA: Newbury House.

Hillyard, L., R. Reppen, and **C. Vásquez.** 2007. 'Bringing the outside world into an intensive English programme.' *ELT Journal* 61/2: 126–34.

Hofstede, G. 1980. *Culture's Consequences: International Differences in Work-Related Values.* Beverly Hills, CA: Sage.

Hoven, D. 1999. 'A model for listening and viewing comprehension in multimedia environments.' *Language Learning and Technology* 3/1: 88–103.

Hudson, T. 1982. 'The effects of induced schemata on the "short circuit" in L2 reading: Non-decoding factors in L2 reading performance.' *Language Learning* 32/1: 1–31.

Hudson, T. 2007. *Teaching Second Language Reading.* Oxford: Oxford University Press.

Hulstijn, J. 2003. 'Connectionist models of language processing and the training of listening skills with the aid of multimedia software.' *Computer Assisted Language Learning* 16/5: 413–25.

IALS. 1997. 'Video self-access: Transcript tasks.' Course materials. Mimeo. Institute for Applied Language Studies, University of Edinburgh.

IALS. 2008. 'Independent study: Introduction.' Course materials. Mimeo. Institute for Applied Language Studies, University of Edinburgh.

Ibarz, T. and **S. Webb.** 2007. 'Listening to learners to investigate the viability of technology-driven ESOL pedagogy.' *Innovation in Language Learning and Teaching* 1/2: 208–26.

James, K., R. Jordan, and **A. Matthews.** 1979. *Listening Comprehension and Note-Taking Course.* London: Collins.

Johnson, P. 1982. 'Effects on reading comprehension of building background knowledge.' *TESOL Quarterly* 16/4: 503–16.

Joiner, E. 1986. 'Listening in the foreign language' in B. H. Wing (ed.). *Listening, Reading and Writing: Analysis and Application.* Middleburgh, VT: North-East Conference on the Teaching of Foreign Languages.

Jordan, R. 1982. *Figures in Language.* Glasgow: Collins.

Kasper, G. 1984. 'Pragmatic comprehension in learner-native speaker discourse.' *Language Learning* 34/1: 1–18.

Kelch, K. 1985. 'Modified input as an aid to comprehension.' *Studies in Second Language Acquisition* 7/1: 81–90.

Kellerman, S. 1990. 'Lip service: The contribution of the visual modality to speech perception and its relevance to the teaching and testing of foreign language listening comprehension.' *Applied Linguistics* 11/3: 272–80.

Kelly, P. 1991. 'Lexical ignorance: The main obstacle to listening comprehension with advanced foreign language learners.' *International Review of Applied Linguistics* XXXIX/2: 135–49.

Kennedy, G. 1978. *The Testing of Listening Comprehension*. RELC monograph. Singapore: Regional English Language Centre.

King, P. and **R. Behnke.** 1989. 'The effect of time-compressed speech on comprehensive, interpretive and short-term listening.' *Human Communication Research* 15: 428–41.

Kissinger, L. 1990. 'Universal worksheets for using with satellite television.' Poster presentation at TESOL Conference, San Francisco, USA, 6–10 March 1990.

Kondo, D. and **Y-L. Yang.** 2004. 'Strategies for coping with language anxiety: The case of students of English in Japan.' *ELT Journal* 58/3: 258–65.

Kramsch, C. 1985. 'Classroom interaction and discourse options.' *Studies in Second Language Acquisition* 7/2: 169–83.

Krashen, S. 1996. 'The case for narrow listening.' *System* 24/1: 97–100.

Lam, W. and **J. Wong.** 2000. 'The effects of strategy training on discussion skills in an ESL classroom.' *ELT Journal* 54/3: 245–55.

Laviosa, F. 2000. 'The listening comprehension processes and strategies of learners of Italian: A case study.' *Rassegna Italiana di Linguistica Applicata* 2: 129–59.

Levelt, W. 1993. 'The architecture of normal spoken language use' in G. Blanken, J. Dittmann, H. Grimm, J. Marshall, and C-W. Wallesch (eds.). *Linguistic Disorders and Pathologies*. Berlin: de Gruyter.

Licklider, J. and **G. Miller.** 1951. 'The perception of speech' in S. Stevens (ed.). *Handbook of Experimental Psychology*. New York, NY: Wiley.

Lightbown, P. and **N. Spada.** 2006. *How Languages are Learned*. 3rd edition. Oxford: Oxford University Press.

Littlejohn, A. 1997. 'Self-access work and curriculum ideologies' in P. Benson and P. Voller (eds.). *Autonomy and Independence in Language Learning*. London: Longman.

Littlewood, W. 1997. 'Self-access: Why do we want it and what can it do?' in P. Benson and P. Voller (eds.). *Autonomy and Independence in Language Learning*. London: Longman.

Long, D. 1990. 'What you don't know can't help you: An exploratory study of background knowledge and second language listening comprehension.' *Studies in Second Language Acquisition* 12/1: 65–80.

Long, M. 1983. 'Linguistic and conversational adjustments to non-native speakers.' *Studies in Second Language Acquisition* 5/2: 177–93.

Long, M. 1985. 'Input and second language acquisition theory' in S. Gass and C. Madden (eds.). *Input in Second Language Acquisition*. Rowley, MA: Newbury House.

Longman Dictionary of the English Language. 1984. Harlow: Longman.

Lund, R. 1991. 'A comparison of second language listening and reading comprehension.' *Modern Language Journal* 75/2: 196–204.

Lynch, T. 1983. 'A programme to develop the integration of comprehension skills.' *ELT Journal* 37/1: 58–61.

Lynch, T. 1988. 'Grading foreign language listening comprehension materials: The use of naturally modified interaction.' PhD thesis, University of Edinburgh.

Lynch, T. 1995. 'The development of interactive listening strategies in second language academic settings' in D. Mendelsohn and J. Rubin (eds.). *A Guide for the Teaching of Second Language Listening*. San Diego, CA: Dominie Press.

Lynch, T. 1996a. *Communication in the Language Classroom*. Oxford: Oxford University Press.

Lynch, T. 1996b. 'The listening–speaking connection.' *English Teaching Professional* 1/1: 10–11.

Lynch, T. 1997. 'Life in the slow lane: Observations of a limited L2 listener.' *System* 25: 385–98.

Lynch, T. 2001. 'Promoting EAP learner autonomy in a second language university context' in J. Flowerdew and M. Peacock (eds.). *Research Perspectives on English for Academic Purposes*. Cambridge: Cambridge University Press.

Lynch, T. 2004. *Study Listening*. 2nd edition. Cambridge: Cambridge University Press.

Lynch, T. 2006. 'Helping university students help themselves to listen.' Keynote paper at BAAL/CUP Seminar on Listening. University of Warwick, May 2006.

Lynch, T. 2007. 'Learning from the transcripts of an oral communication task.' *ELT Journal* 61/4: 311–20.

Lynch, T. 2009a. 'The Speaking Log: A tool for post-task feedback' in T. Stewart (ed.). *Insights on Teaching Speaking*. Alexandria, VA: TESOL.

Lynch, T. 2009b. 'Responding to learners' perceptions of feedback: The use of comparators in second language speaking courses.' Available online at http://dx.doi.org/10.1080/17501220802379109. *Innovation in Language Learning and Teaching 3/2*.

Mace, W. 1977. 'James J. Gibson's strategy for perceiving: Ask not what's inside your head but what your head's inside of' in R. Shaw and J. Bransford (eds.). *Perceiving, Acting and Knowing*. Hillsdale, NJ: Lawrence Erlbaum.

Mackey, M. 2002. *Literacies across the Media: Playing the Text*. London: Routledge Falmer.

Maley, A. 1983. 'The teaching of listening comprehension skills' in S. Holden (ed.). *Second Selections from Modern English Teacher*. London: Longman.

Markham, P. 2001. 'The influence of culture-specific background knowledge and captions on second language comprehension.' *Journal of Educational Technology Systems* 29/4: 331–43.

Markham, P. and **M. Latham.** 1987. 'The influence of religion-specific background knowledge on the listening comprehension of adult second-language students.' *Language Learning* 37/2: 157–70.

Mason, A. 1994. 'By dint of: Student and lecturer perceptions of lecture comprehension strategies in first-term graduate study' in J. Flowerdew (ed.). *Academic Listening: Research Perspectives*. Cambridge: Cambridge University Press.

McCarthy, M. 1991. *Discourse Analysis for Language Teachers*. Cambridge: Cambridge University Press.

McDonough, S. 1976. 'Listening comprehension: The effect of test questions on delayed recognition of content and expressions.' *Audio Visual Language Journal* 14/3: 147–52.

McDonough, S. 2006. 'Learner strategies: An interview with Steve McDonough.' *ELT Journal* 60/1: 63–70.

McGrath, I. 2002. *Materials Evaluation and Design for Language Teaching*. Edinburgh: Edinburgh University Press.

McGurk, H. and **J. MacDonald.** 1976. 'Hearing lips and seeing voices.' *Nature* 264: 746–8.

Mecartty, F. 2000. 'Lexical and grammatical knowledge in reading and listening comprehension by foreign language learners of Spanish.' *Applied Language Learning* 11/2: 323–48.

Meinhof, U. 1998. *Language Learning in the Age of Satellite Television.* Oxford: Oxford University Press.

Mendelsohn, D. 1994. *Learning to Listen: A Strategy-based Approach for the Second-language Learner.* San Diego, CA: Dominie Press.

Mendelsohn, D. 1995. 'Applying learning strategies in the second/foreign language listening comprehension lesson' in D. Mendelsohn and J. Rubin (eds.). *A Guide for the Teaching of Second Language Listening.* San Diego, CA: Dominie Press.

Mendelsohn, D. 1998. 'Teaching listening.' *Annual Review of Applied Linguistics* 18: 81–101.

Miller, L., E. Tsang, and **M. Hopkins.** 2007. 'Establishing a self-access centre in a secondary school.' *ELT Journal* 61/3: 220–7.

Morrison, B. 2008. 'The role of the self-access centre in the tertiary language learning process.' *System* 36/2: 123–40.

Neisser, U. 1976. *Cognition and Reality.* San Francisco: Freeman.

Nunan, D. 1991. *Language Teaching Methodology.* Hemel Hempstead: Prentice Hall.

Nunan, D. 1997. 'Designing and adapting materials to encourage learner autonomy' in P. Benson and P. Voller (eds.). *Autonomy and Independence in Language Learning.* London: Longman.

Nuttall, C. 1982. *Teaching Reading Skills in a Foreign Language.* Oxford: Heinemann.

Nuttall, C. 1996. *Teaching Reading Skills in a Foreign Language.* 2nd edition. Oxford: Heinemann.

Ochs, E. 1979. 'Planned and unplanned discourse' in T. Givon (ed.). *Syntax and Semantics Volume 12: Discourse and Syntax.* New York: Academic Press.

Oller, J. 1979. *Language Tests at School.* London: Longman.

O'Malley, J., A. Chamot, and **L. Küpper.** 1989. 'Listening comprehension strategies in second language acquisition.' *Applied Linguistics* 10/4: 418–37.

O'Neill, R. and **R. Scott.** 1974. *Viewpoints.* Harlow: Longman.

Oprandy, R. 1994. 'Listening/speaking in second and foreign language teaching.' *System* 22/2: 153–75.

Oxford, R. 1990. *Language Learning Strategies: What Every Teacher Should Know.* New York: Newbury House.

Oxford, R. (ed.).1996. *Language Learning Strategies Around the World: Cross-Cultural Perspectives.* Manoa, HW: University of Hawaii Press.

Oxford, R. 2002. 'Sources of variation in language learning' in R. Kaplan (ed.). *Oxford Handbook of Applied Linguistics.* Oxford: Oxford University Press.

Oxford, R. and **A. Cohen.** 1992. 'Language learning strategies: Crucial issues of concept and classification.' *Applied Language Learning* 3/1: 1–35.

Oxford, R. and **N. Anderson.** 1995. 'A cross-cultural view of learning styles.' *Language Teaching* 28: 201–15.

Paredes, R., H. Ogata, N. Saito, C. Yin, Y. Yano, Y. Oishi, and **T. Ueda.** 2005. 'LOCH: Supporting informal language learning outside the classroom with handhelds.' *Proceedings of the 2005 IEEE International Workshop on Wireless and Mobile Technologies in Education (WMTE '05).* Available online at http://ieeexplore.ieee.org/ie15/10547/33360/01579261.pdf

Pica T., R. Young, and **C. Doughty.** 1987. 'The impact of interaction on comprehension.' *TESOL Quarterly* 21/4: 737–58.

Price, K. 1983. 'Closed-captioned TV: An untapped resource.' *MATESOL Newsletter* 12: 1–8.

Pujolà, J-T. 2007. 'Cooperative audiovisual comprehension using Web 2.0 tools.' Paper presented at Eurocall 2007. Coleraine, Northern Ireland.

Ramírez Verdugo, D. and **I. Alonso Belmonte.** 2007. 'Using digital stories to improve listening comprehension with Spanish young learners.' *Language Learning and Technology* 11/1: 87–101.

Rees-Miller, J. 1993. 'A critical appraisal of learner training: Theoretical bases and teaching implications.' *TESOL Quarterly* 27/4: 679–89.

Richards, J. 1983. 'Listening comprehension: Approach, design, procedure.' *TESOL Quarterly* 17/2: 219–40.

Richards, J. 2006. 'Materials development and research—making the connection.' *RELC Journal* 37/1: 5–26.

Richards, J. 2007. 'Materials development and research: Towards a form-focused perspective' in S. Fotos and H. Nassaji (eds.). *Form-Focused Instruction and Teacher Education.* Oxford: Oxford University Press.

Ridgway, T. 2000. 'Listening strategies—I beg your pardon?' *ELT Journal* 54/2: 179–85.

Riley, P. 1981. 'Viewing comprehension: L'oeil écoute' in British Council: *The Teaching of Listening Comprehension.* Oxford: Pergamon/British Council.

Riley, P. 1997. 'The guru and the conjurer: Aspects of counselling for self-access' in P. Benson and P. Voller (eds.). *Autonomy and Independence in Language Learning.* London: Longman.

Robb, T. and **B. Susser.** 1989. 'Extensive reading versus skills building in an EFL context.' *Reading in a Foreign Language* 5/2: 239–52.

Robin, R. 2007. 'Learner-based listening and technological authenticity.' *Language Learning and Technology* 11/1: 109–15.

Roberts, C. 1996. 'A social perspective on understanding: Some issues of theory and method' in K. Bremer, C. Roberts, M. Vasseur, M. Simonot, and P. Broeder (eds.). *Achieving Understanding: Discourse in International Encounters.* London: Longman.

Ross, S. 1997. 'An introspective analysis of listener inferencing on a second language listening test' in G. Kasper and E. Kellerman (eds.). *Communication Strategies: Psycholinguistic and Sociolinguistic Perspectives.* London: Longman.

Rost, M. 1990. *Listening in Language Learning.* London: Longman.

Rost, M. 2002. *Teaching and Researching Listening.* London: Longman.

Rost, M. 2006. 'Areas of research that influence L2 listening instruction' in E. Usó-Juan and A. Martínez-Flor (eds.). *Current Trends in the Development and Teaching of the Four Language Skills.* Berlin: Mouton de Gruyter.

Rost, M. 2007. 'Commentary: *I'm only trying to help*: A role for interventions in teaching listening.' *Language Learning and Technology* 11/1: 102–8.

Rost, M. and **S. Ross.** 1991. 'Learner use of strategies in interaction: Typology and teachability.' *Language Learning* 41/2: 235–73.

Rubin, J. 1995. 'The contribution of video to the development of competence in listening' in D. Mendelsohn and J. Rubin (eds.). *A Guide for the Teaching of Second Language Listening.* San Diego, CA: Dominie Press.

Rubin, J. and **I. Thompson.** 1982. *How to Be a Successful Language Learner.* New York: Heinle and Heinle.

Ryan, S. 1997. 'Preparing learners for independence: Resources beyond the classroom' in P. Benson and P. Voller (eds.). *Autonomy and Independence in Language Learning.* Harlow: Longman.

Sacks, H. 1971. 'Mimeo lecture notes' cited in M. Coulthard 1977: *An Introduction to Discourse Analysis.* Harlow: Longman.

Salaberry, M. 2001. 'The use of technology for second language learning and teaching: A retrospective.' *Modern Language Journal* 85/1: 39–56.

Samuda, V. 2001. 'Guiding relationships between form and meaning during task performance: The role of the teacher' in M. Bygate, P. Skehan, and M. Swain (eds.). *Researching Pedagogic Tasks: Second Language Learning, Teaching and Testing.* Harlow: Pearson Education.

Schmidt, R. and **S. Frota.** 1986. 'Developing basic conversational ability in a second language: A case study of an adult learner of Portuguese' in R. Day (ed.). *Talking to Learn: Conversation in Second Language Acquisition.* Rowley, MA: Newbury House.

Schmidt-Rinehart, B. 1994. 'The effects of topic familiarity on second language listening comprehension.' *Modern Language Journal* 78/2: 179–89.

Schumann, J. 2001. 'Learning as foraging' in Z. Dörnyei and R. Schmidt (eds.). *Motivation and Second Language Acquisition.* Technical Report 23. Honolulu: University of Hawaii.

Seedhouse, P. 1996. 'Classroom interaction: Possibilities and impossibilities.' *ELT Journal* 50/1: 16–24.

Shannon, C. 1949. 'The mathematical theory of communication' in C. Shannon and W. Weaver (eds.). *The Mathematical Theory of Communication.* Urbana, IL: University of Illinois.

Shannon, C. and **W. Weaver** (eds.). 1949. *The Mathematical Theory of Communication.* Urbana, IL: University of Illinois.

Sheerin, S. 1989. *Self-Access.* Oxford: Oxford University Press.

Sherman, J. 1998. 'Independent vocabulary learning.' *IATEFL Issues* June–July 1998: 14–15.

Shohamy, E. and **O. Inbar**. 1991. 'Validation of listening comprehension tests: The effect of text and question type.' *Language Testing* 8/1: 23–40.

Sperber, D. and **D. Wilson.** 1995. *Relevance: Communication and Cognition.* 2nd edition. Oxford: Blackwell.

Spolsky, B. 1994. 'Comprehension testing, or can understanding be measured?' in G. Brown, K. Malmkjaer, A. Pollitt, and J. Williams (eds.). *Language and Understanding.* Oxford: Oxford University Press.

Sticht, T. and **J. James.** 1984. 'Listening and reading' in D. Pearson (ed.). *Handbook of Reading Research.* New York: Longman.

Swain, M. and **S. Lapkin.** 1995. 'Problems in output and the cognitive processes they generate: A step towards second language learning.' *Applied Linguistics* 16/3: 371–91.

Tannen, D. 1982. *Spoken and Written Language: Exploring Orality and Literacy.* Norwood, NJ: Ablex.

Tarone, E. and **G. Yule.** 1989. *Focus on the Language Learner.* Oxford: Oxford University Press.

Tauroza, S. 1995. 'Trouble shooting' in D. Nunan and L. Miller (eds.). *New Ways in Teaching Listening.* Alexandria, VA: TESOL.

Thompson, I. 1993. 'An investigation of the effects of texts and tasks on listening comprehension: Some evidence from Russian.' *Georgetown University Round Table on Languages and Linguistics.* Washington, DC: Georgetown University Press.

Thompson, I. 1995. 'Assessment of second/foreign language listening comprehension' in D. Mendelsohn and J. Rubin (eds.). *A Guide for the Teaching of Second Language Listening.* San Diego, CA: Dominie Press.

Thornbury, S. and **D. Slade.** 2006. *Conversation: From Description to Pedagogy.* Cambridge: Cambridge University Press.

Tsui, A. and **J. Fullilove.** 1998. 'Bottom-up or top-down processing as a discriminator of L2 listening performance.' *Applied Linguistics* 19/4: 432–51.

Tudor, I. 1996. *Learner-centredness as Language Education.* Cambridge: Cambridge University Press.

Tyler, M. 2001. 'Resource consumption as a function of topic knowledge in non-native and native comprehension.' *Language Learning* 51/2: 257–80.

Underwood, M. 1971. *Listen to This!* Oxford: Oxford University Press.

Underwood, M. 1976. *What a Story!* Oxford: Oxford University Press.

Underwood, M. 1979. *Have You Heard?* Oxford: Oxford University Press.

van Dijk, T. and **W. Kintsch.** 1983. *Strategies of Discourse Comprehension.* New York: Academic Press.

van Lier, L. 2000. 'From input to affordance: Social-interactive learning from an ecological perspective' in J. Lantolf (ed.). *Sociocultural Theory and Second Language Learning.* Oxford: Oxford University Press.

Vandergrift, L. 1999. 'Facilitating second language listening comprehension: Acquiring successful strategies.' *ELT Journal* 53/3: 168–76.

Vandergrift, L. 2003. 'Orchestrating strategy use: Toward a model of the skilled second language listener.' *Language Learning* 53/3: 463–96.

Vandergrift, L. 2004. 'Listening to learn or learning to listen?' *Annual Review of Applied Linguistics* 24: 3–25.

Vandergrift, L. 2006. 'Second language listening: Listening ability or language proficiency?' *Modern Language Journal* 90/1: 6–18.

Vandergrift, L. 2007. 'Recent developments in second and foreign language listening research.' *Language Teaching* 40: 191–210.

Vandergrift, L., C. Goh, C. Mareschal, and **M. Tafaghodtari.** 2006. 'The metacognitive awareness listening questionnaire: development and validation.' *Language Learning* 56/3: 431–62.

Vanderplank, R. 1988. 'The value of teletext sub-titles in language learning.' *ELT Journal* 42/3: 272–81.

Vanderplank, R. 1993. 'Pacing and spacing as predictors of difficulty in speaking and understanding English.' *ELT Journal* 47/2: 117–25.

Varonis, M. and **S. Gass.** 1985. 'Non-native/non-native conversations: A model for the negotiation of meaning.' *Applied Linguistics* 6/1: 71–90.

Vogely, A. 1999. 'Addressing listening comprehension anxiety' in D. Young (ed.). *Affect in FL and SL Learning: A Practical Guide to Creating a Low-Anxiety Classroom Atmosphere.* New York: McGraw Hill.

Voss, B. 1984. 'Perception of first-language and second-language texts: A comparative study.' *Bielefelder Beiträge zur Sprachlehrforschung* 13/2: 131–53.

Vygotsky, L. 1978. *Mind in Society: The Development of Higher Psychological Processes.* Cambridge, MA: Harvard University Press.

Wajnryb, R. 1990. *Grammar Dictation.* Oxford: Oxford University Press.

Waring, R. 2006. 'Extensive listening materials.' Available at http://www.robwaring.org/el/. Accessed 12 September 2008.

Whitaker, S. 1983. 'Comprehension questions: About face!' *ELT Journal* 37/4: 329–34.

White, G. 1998. *Listening.* Oxford: Oxford University Press.

Widdowson, H. G. 1979. *Explorations in Applied Linguistics 1.* Oxford: Oxford University Press.

Williams, H. and **D. Thorne.** 2000. 'The value of teletext subtitling as a medium for language learning.' *System* 28/2: 217–28.

Windsor Lewis, J. 1969. *A Guide to English Pronunciation.* Oslo: Universitetsforlaget.

Wolff, D. 1987. 'Some assumptions about second language text comprehension.' *Studies in Second Language Acquisition* 9/3: 307–26.

Yo, I. 2006. 'The effects of test anxiety in listening test performance.' *System* 34/3: 317–40.

Yule, G. 1997. *Referential Communication Tasks*. Mahwah, NJ: Lawrence Erlbaum.

Yule, G. and **M. Powers.** 1994. 'Investigating the communicative outcomes of task-based interaction.' *System* 22/1: 81–91.

Zielinski, B. 2008. 'The listener: No longer the silent partner in intelligibility.' *System* 36/1: 69–84.

INDEX

Oxford Handbooks for Language Teachers

This series is designed to provide a source of reference for both language teachers and teacher trainers. Each title is intended to serve both as a basis for courses and seminars, and as a longer-term reference text for the working teacher's bookshelf.

How Languages are Learned

THIRD EDITION

Patsy M. Lightbown and Nina Spada

A thoroughly updated edition of this prize-winning, readable introduction to the main theories of first and second language acquisition.

- Relates theories of first and second language acquisition to classroom methodology and practice.

New for this edition:

- Explores recent theories such as skill learning, connectionism, and the 'noticing hypothesis'.
- Includes more on current theories of first language acquisition and early bilingualism, and factors affecting learning such as motivation and learning styles.
- Includes a greater variety of ethnic, cultural, and linguistic backgrounds in a fully revised classroom learning section.

PATSY LIGHTBOWN is Distinguished Emeritus Professor of Applied Linguistics at Concordia University, Montreal.

NINA SPADA is Professor in the Department of Curriculum Teaching and Learning, Modern Language Centre, OISE/University of Toronto.

Reviews of previous editions:

❢ A sensible book mercifully free of jargon. ❢
Panel of judges, Duke of Edinburgh Book Competition

❢ How Languages are Learned is an absolute "must have" for every teachers' room, and I would go so far as to say, if a teacher reads only one ELT book in the next six months, this should be the one. ❢
ELT News, Japan

You can buy this book online at www.oup.com/elt

For further information please contact your local OUP office or write to:

ELT Marketing Communications
Oxford University Press
Great Clarendon Street
Oxford
OX2 6DP
UK

Email: elt.enquiry@oup.com
www.oup.com/elt

978 0 19 442224 6

OXFORD
UNIVERSITY PRESS

Some other titles available in the Oxford Handbooks for Language Teachers series ...

Task-Based Teaching

SHORTLISTED FOR THE BEN WARREN PRIZE

Dave Willis and Jane Willis

978 0 19 442210 9

❝ I would strongly recommend this book to teachers and teacher trainers for its very clear and practical advice on how to make effective classroom use of task-based approaches ❞

Brian Tomlinson, ELT Journal

The Oxford ESOL Handbook

Philida Schellekens

❝ At last! A book which directly addresses ESOL practitioners ... giving teachers the practical tools to enhance their pedagogy and enrich the experience of learner and teacher alike. ❞

Modern English Teacher

978 0 19 442281 9

ESOL: A Critical Guide

James Cooke and Melanie Simpson

❝ This book is a must read for all ESOL education specialists on initial teacher education, CPD, and MA courses. ❞

Helen Sunderland, London South Bank University

978 0 19 442267 3

From Experience to Knowledge in ELT

Julian Edge and Sue Garton

978 0 19 442271 0

Communication in the Language Classroom

Tony Lynch

978 0 19 433522 5

Explaining English Grammar

SHORTLISTED FOR THE BEN WARREN PRIZE

George Yule

978 0 19 437172 8

Doing Second Language Research

James Dean Brown and Theodore S. Rodgers

978 0 19 437174 2

Teaching Second Language Reading

Thom D. Hudson

978 0 19 442283 3

For a full list of Oxford Handbooks for Language Teachers and a range of inspiring ideas, resources, and support for teachers, visit www.oup.com/elt

OXFORD
UNIVERSITY PRESS

Oxford Introductions to Language Study

For training courses, academic study, and teachers with a thirst for knowledge. 15 titles available.

SMALL BOOKS. BIG IDEAS

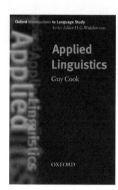

❝ ... very readable with many concrete examples. ❞
EL Gazette

❝ ... accessible without being superficial. ❞
SATEFL Newsletter

NEW Translation
Juliane House

NEW Semantics
A.P. Cowie

Discourse Analysis
H. G. Widdowson

Grammar
Michael Swan

Applied Linguistics
Guy Cook

Stylistics
Peter Verdonk

Phonetics
Peter Roach

Historical Linguistics
Herbert Schendl

Language and Culture
Claire Kramsch

Language Testing
Tim McNamara

Psycholinguistics
Tom Scovel

Pragmatics
George Yule

Second Language Acquisition
Rod Ellis

Sociolinguistics
Bernard Spolsky

Linguistics
H. G. Widdowson

OXFORD
UNIVERSITY PRESS

Oxford Applied Linguistics

NEW discussions from the world's leading Applied
Linguistics series

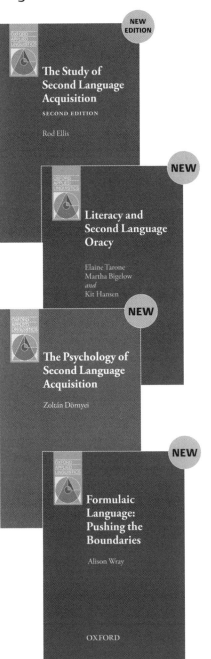

❋ What are the major perspectives encompassed in the field of second language acquisition research today?

❋ How does low literacy affect how language learners understand oral input?

❋ How do linguistics and theories of psychology converge in recent research on second language acquisition?

❋ What happens when language users favour formulaic language over something more spontaneous?

Find out more at www.oup.com/elt